RECORD OF THE
4TH ROYAL IRISH DRAGOON GUARDS
IN THE GREAT WAR
1914-1918

RECORD OF THE 4TH ROYAL IRISH DRAGOON GUARDS IN THE GREAT WAR 1914–1918

BY THE

REV. HAROLD GIBB

LIEUT. 4TH R. I. DRAGOON GUARDS
1914–1915

1925

CANTERBURY

CONTENTS

FOREWORD

MY old friend and comrade in arms, Major-General Mullens, has asked me to write a Foreword to this Record of the 4th Royal Irish Dragoon Guards in the Great War ; and I gladly comply.

General Mullens had the rare good fortune to train the Regiment in Peace and to command it in the Field.

Before the War I watched the training of the Regiment, under his able guidance ; and I was confident that, if war came, the 4th Dragoon Guards would well uphold the great name of our Cavalry. I was not mistaken.

From the moment when, on the 22nd August, 1914, Corporal Thomas fired the first shot, until the Armistice, more than four years later, the 4th Dragoon Guards played a part which has won for them a place high on the roll of fame.

In this book, the tale of their great deeds is simply and clearly recorded.

ALLENBY.

F.M.

CAIRO,
17th May, 1923.

PREFACE

IN presenting the Record of the 4th Royal Irish Dragoon Guards in the European War, 1914–1918, to those now serving, those yet to serve, past members, and friends of the Regiment, the Editor wishes to express regret for the delay in publication.

Grateful acknowledgment is made to Sir Henry Newbolt for allowing the insertion of his poem, " The Toy Band," also of the loan of diaries by Officers, while accuracy in the compilation of the narrative and appendices, together with the general production, would have been quite impossible under the circumstances, through loss of eyesight, but for the careful assistance of Mr. K. R. Wilson.

It is hoped that the Biographical Notes will be of value for reference, and will in some degree make up for the lack of personal incidents in the narrative, which, owing to the want of the necessary material, have unavoidably not been included.

The object of this little book will have been achieved if it is appreciated by the Officers, N.C.O.'s, and Privates of the 4th Royal Irish Dragoon Guards, as a faithful record of the Regiment throughout the Great War.

HAROLD GIBB.

June, 1923.

MEMORANDUM

BY

LIEUT.-GENERAL SIR E. C. BETHUNE, K.C.B., C.V.O.

WHILE the Regiment was fighting during the Great War, there was little that we could do on the Home Front, except to do what we could to look after the dependants of the men who might be in trouble. A special war fund was raised and administered by the Cavalry Benefit Association, to which the Regiment is affiliated. We all owe a great debt of gratitude to Miss Cross and the Staff of that Association for all the splendid work they did during those trying years. The comfort of the unfortunate Prisoners of War was looked after by Mrs. Fuller, who worked extremely hard.

Later the prisoners' food parcels and gifts were administered through the Irish Women's Association, our interests being supervised by Mrs. Rickards, who all through the war worked with untiring zeal.

Gifts were continually forwarded to the Regiment. These consisted of every kind of useful thing, from cigarettes and tobacco to footballs, jerseys, and books, etc., and warm clothing. Mrs. Oppenheim was specially generous in sending large quantities of clothing, which were found exceedingly useful. Wives and dependants of men on service were helped in money and in kind, and everything was done that our funds allowed to ease the position of our men abroad.

EDWARD C. BETHUNE,
Colonel, 4th (R.I.) Dragoon Guards.

FIELD-MARSHAL VISCOUNT ALLENBY, G.C.B., G.C.M.G.,
G.O.C.
THE CAVALRY CORPS,
B.E.F.
(FRANCE)

THE
4TH
ROYAL IRISH
DRAGOON GUARDS

CHAPTER I

1914

MONS

ON the declaration of war the 4th Dragoon Guards were stationed at Tidworth, Salisbury Plain, occupying Assaye Barracks, and, together with the 9th Lancers and the 18th Hussars, formed the 2nd Cavalry Brigade under the command of Brig.-General H. de B. de Lisle, C.B., D.S.O.

The Cavalry Division, under the command of Major-General E. H. H. Allenby, C.B., was composed of:—

1ST CAVALRY BRIGADE.
(Brig.-General C. J. Briggs, C.B.)
2nd Dragoon Guards.
5th Dragoon Guards.
11th Hussars.
" J," " I," " L " Batteries R.H.A.

2ND CAVALRY BRIGADE.
(Brig.-General H. de B. de Lisle, C.B.)
4th Dragoon Guards.
9th Lancers.
18th Hussars.
" H," " K " Batteries R.H.A.

3RD CAVALRY BRIGADE.
(Brig.-General H. de la P. Gough, C.B.)
4th Hussars.
5th Lancers.
16th Lancers.
" D," " E " Batteries R.H.A.

1

4TH CAVALRY BRIGADE.
(Brig.-General the Hon. C. E. Bingham, C.V.O., C.B.)
6th Dragoon Guards.
3rd Hussars.
Household Cavalry Composite Regiment.
Q.O. Oxfordshire Hussars.
" P," " R," " C " Batteries R.H.A.

5TH CAVALRY BRIGADE.
(Brig.-General Sir P. W. Chetwode, Bart., D.S.O.)
Royal Scots Greys.
12th Lancers.
20th Hussars.
" G," " O " Batteries R.H.A.

The Regiment left Tidworth for Southampton, embarking at noon on H.M.T. *Winifredian* on August 15, 1914, and disembarked at Boulogne the following day. After a few days in Rest Camp, Haupmont was reached by train on the 19th. Marching via Damousies and Harmignies, the Brigade was pushed forward to hold Bois la Haut, a position south-east of Mons.

No contact having been established with the enemy, " C " Squadron, under Major Bridges, was sent forward in advance of the Cavalry Division with orders to act as " contact " Squadron, and gain information of the direction and forces of the enemy, and to capture prisoners if possible.

The Squadron moved forward to St. Denis, halting there for the night. Patrols were sent out and the surroundings picketed. During the afternoon so many elements, apparently hostile, in plain clothes on bicycles were seen, that Major Bridges decided to move the Squadron as soon as it became dark. This was done, moving south-west about a mile to some high ground in a cornfield, where it remained till just before dawn.

August 22.

Several patrols were sent out during the night and did some good work, notably those under Lieutenants Harrison, Aylmer, and Jones, and Corporal Savoury. The gist of the information received, obtained from various sources—fugitives and residents from the surrounding country, including a retired General— led Major Bridges to the conclusion that the Germans were pouring south on every road from Brussels, and that their numbers

must be at least 400,000 on this front. This information was
sent back to the Cavalry Division, which it reached on the
morning of the 22nd. This was the first information that the
Commander-in-Chief received that he was so seriously menaced
in this direction. Just before dawn, the Squadron moved forward
to a wood about a mile away, on a commanding position. Here
Major Bridges sent out a few Cossack Posts and awaited developments in the hope of being able to pick up a German patrol
or two. Nothing, however, was seen, and at about 6.30 a.m.
it was decided to push forward along the main road towards
Soignies, and contact was definitely established with the head
of the German column on that road. The main road was struck
at the little village of Casteau, where the Squadron halted in
concealment, while scouts were sent on. They reported a
German patrol in sight, coming down the road; our patrol
was directed by signal to move straight back towards the south,
to draw on the Germans. Two Troops were dismounted ready
to open fire, the other two Troops drew swords ready to pursue.
About six German Dragoons were seen coming cautiously
down the road. At about five hundred yards from the am-
bush, they apparently smelt a rat, stopped and consulted, and
then turned round and slowly went away. At this moment
the first shot by the British Army in the war was fired
by Corporal Thomas, " C " Squadron. Captain Hornby, thinking he could catch them, asked for permission to try, and was
ordered to charge with the two mounted Troops. This was
done straight down the main road, which was paved and tram-
lined, being about thirty yards in width, with a ditch on either
side. Captain Hornby had with him in the gallop the 1st
Troop of " C " Squadron, under Staff-Sergeant-Major Sharpe,
and one or two men of the 4th Troop. Meanwhile Major
Bridges followed up in support, with the remainder of the
Squadron now mounted. Captain Hornby soon found himself
up against a German Squadron which was following their
scouts. This also turned and fled. A chase followed for
about one and a half miles. During the pursuit, the Uhlans
were joined by one or two Troops of Hussars who swelled the
rout. The leading troops, under Captain Hornby, came up to
them at the bottom of a slight hill. The men cheered and
drove right in amongst them, sabring several and dismounting
many, who were taken prisoners. Many of the Germans threw

away their long lances during the fight, and tried to surrender, but did not get much opportunity.

There was some shooting out of windows of houses by the roadside during this mêlée. The remnants were pursued till Captain Hornby was brought up by rifle fire from troops deployed across the road. Captain Hornby led his men into the enclosure of a château, and returned the fire. The other two Troops were brought up in support. Some light transport was obtained from an English trainer who lived close by, and who had been cheering our troops as they passed through ; carts were requisitioned to get away prisoners who had been taken, and several of our own men whose horses had been shot. Major Bridges concluded that he was up against the head of a German Cavalry Division, as cyclists were to be seen and entrenchments in front of our position on a hill about four hundred yards off.

Our object having been obtained, it was decided to withdraw the Squadron as rapidly as possible to avoid being outflanked and cut off. Captain Hornby moved off at the trot, while his retirement was covered by Major Bridges with the two other Troops. The retirement being carried out, a message was despatched to the General Officer Commanding Cavalry Division to the effect that, if Major Bridges could be given a couple or more Squadrons, he thought he could manœuvre round the right flank of the enemy and inflict considerable damage on the Germans, whose morale was evidently not very high.

Orders were, however, received to rejoin the Cavalry Division, as other plans had been made. The enemy had apparently been given a severe fright, as there were no further symptoms of an attempt to advance down the main road during the rest of the day.

This was the first contact in the war between the British and the Germans. It was within a few miles of this same spot that the 4th Dragoon Guards were fighting at the moment of the signing of the Armistice on November 11, 1918. Captain Hornby was the first officer to draw blood, and according to a promise made by the Brigadier at Tidworth, was recommended and awarded the D.S.O., having been brought to notice for conspicuous gallantry.

The Cavalry Division, elated at their first sight of German prisoners, gave the Squadron a rousing reception on their return. The Brigadier issued the following Operation Order in connection with this engagement :—

The Brigadier desires to congratulate the 4th Dragoon Guards on the spirited action of two Troops of the Squadron on reconnaissance, which resulted in establishing the moral superiority of our cavalry from the first, over the German cavalry."

During the first few days of the war the operations undertaken by the cavalry were in the gap between the First and Second Armies.

The objective of the British Army was to prevent an outflanking movement by the Germans on the Western front of the French line; the first on-rush of the German Army was met by the Belgians on this side, while the arrival of the British Expeditionary Force strengthened the position. The outflanking movement of the Germans frustrated, the attack was concentrated along the whole N.W. front. In co-operation with the plans of the French Army Commanders, Sir John French withdrew his Army from its forward position to a more Southern line along the Le Cateau-Cambrai main road.

So began the Retreat on Paris, a movement contested day by day, until the opportune moment arrived for the French and British Armies to make the offensive. " Retreat " is never a pleasant word to a soldier, still more so when the reason for it is obscure, and the position on one's immediate front seems not to justify it. Such was the position at this time, but the policy of the High Command had been decided upon, and it was undoubtedly influenced by the condition of the country around Maubeuge, where fighting was made difficult by standing crops.

The time necessary for consolidation of the French South and South-West fronts had been gained by the arrival of the British Expeditionary Force, and the stemming of the German on-rush. The more difficult rôle now followed to withdraw before the enemy ; that of the cavalry being to cover the retreat, to contest every inch of ground, and above all to be in perfect trim to take the offensive when the right moment arrived.

It will be for ever to the credit and glory of the British Expeditionary Force that this was achieved, and eventually on September 5, when in spite of the strain of the long retreat, the Expeditionary Force was found ready to press an offensive and drive the enemy back across the Rivers Marne and Aisne, and eventually take up a new front in Flanders and enter on a protracted period of trench-warfare.

CHAPTER II

AUDREGNIES

August 24.

THE 2nd Cavalry Brigade, which had been till now patrolling the gap which existed between the First and Second Army Corps, was now withdrawn, together with the rest of the Cavalry Division, and swung across to the left of the British Army to cover that flank.

A position was taken up along the two roads running north and south through Thulin to Audregnies, to help to cover the retirement of the infantry to take up their new positions by the latter village. Here General de Lisle was ordered to relieve the pressure on the 5th Division, as the result of an urgent call for assistance from General Sir Charles Fergusson.

The 18th Hussars were sent to patrol the Quievrain-Elogies Road, while the 4th Dragoon Guards and the 9th Lancers, at the moment in Audregnies, were to meet the advance of the Germans, coming on in great numbers from the direction of Quievrain to Audregnies. If necessity arose, the cavalry were to charge. The 4th Dragoon Guards made their exit from the north of the village with the 9th Lancers on their right. Intervening ground between the advancing Germans and ourselves consisted of stubble fields in which the corn was in " stooks." Colonel Mullens led the Regiment from the outskirts of the village down a narrow lane between a wall and a high bank, at the end of which was a cottage commanding the exit in the direction of the enemy. Two Troops of " B " Squadron, under Lieutenants Fetherstonhaugh and Hickman, were swept off by heavy rifle and shell fire when trying to occupy the cottage, being forced to take cover to the right of the lane, eventually joining up with the 9th Lancers when that Regiment charged the German position. Major Bridges, to support " B " Squadron, galloped down the

6

lane to occupy the cottage. As they came up to it Major Bridges at the head of his Squadron was struck by shrapnel, brought down with his horse, and narrowly escaped being galloped over by the charging Squadron. Rolling himself to the side of the road, he lay unconscious till picked up, and was taken to the cottage. Meanwhile Major Hunter had been sent to assist " C " Squadron, but " A " Squadron too was driven off by a torrent of fire, and, together with some of the rear troops of " C " Squadron, swept out to the open country to the right.

By the occupation of the cottage and the securing of the position in the lane the advance of the enemy had been held up on the north-west side of the village. The German infantry, however, continued to try to advance. This was shown by Major Bridges' account of his experiences on regaining consciousness and finding himself an inmate of the cottage, with some twenty wounded men. He says : " Two bandsmen were rendering first aid and somebody was pouring water over my head. I got one of the men to help me on to a chair, where I could stand and look through the fanlight over the door, all the windows being shuttered. Bullets were pattering against the walls, and shells flying overhead. I saw line upon line of enemy infantry advancing with fixed bayonets, their nearest scouts not being more than a hundred yards from the cottage. Without a second's thought I decided to get away before it was too late, and rolled out of the window at the back of the house. Here I found rather a shambles of men and horses in the road. There was a chestnut horse with a wound in the shoulder standing patiently among the gooseberry bushes in the garden. I struggled on to his back and ambled off at a slow canter, pursued by a hot fire which, however, did not touch us. In front of me I could see Farrier-Sergeant Old just disappearing into the village. I saw him do some very excellent work pulling wounded men under cover, and have a hazy recollection of being helped into a house by him. Later, Old and I joined up again in the village, and made our way out of it along the railway line on to the hill behind. Here I rested in the garden of a little *estaminet* and could see various bodies of our cavalry collecting themselves in the distance."

While the lane was being secured the other two Troops of " B " Squadron, under Major Hutchison, had come into dismounted action on the north outskirts of the village, and came under heavy shell fire. The casualties on this day, the first on which the Regiment had been subjected to combined heavy rifle and gun fire, amounted to eighty-one (see Casualty List, Appendix III). Major G. T. M. Bridges, D.S.O., Lieutenant Jones, 13th Hussars, attached 4th Dragoon Guards, Major C. F. Hunter and Farrier-Sergeant Old were brought to notice of higher authority for their work in this engagement. Lieutenants A. Gallaher and Hickman, Sergeants Hynes, Gardener, and Bird, and Private Weelgan and others, were taken prisoners.

Special Brigade Order by Brig.-General H. de B. de Lisle, C.B., D.S.O. :—

"Headquarters, 2nd Cavalry Brigade,
August 28, '14.

I wish to express to the 2nd Cavalry Brigade my extreme pride and satisfaction with their conduct in the severe engagement at Audregnies on Monday, August 24.

" The fight was necessary to save the Vth Division from an organized counter-attack during their retirement, and the object was achieved by the gallant and steady conduct of the Brigade. Major-General Sir Charles Fergusson, Commanding Vth Division, thanked me personally for saving his Division, adding that but for the Cavalry Brigade his Division would have been destroyed to the last man. I specially wish to commend the true cavalry spirit of the 9th Lancers, in daring to charge unbroken infantry in order to save neighbouring troops, and that of the 4th Dragoon Guards in the effective support given, without hesitation or thought of danger. I intend to bring to the notice of high authority how greatly I value the devotion of my Brigade."

CHAPTER III

THE RETREAT FROM MONS

THE action at Audregnies resulted in the Regiment being very much scattered, and darkness coming on made it impossible to reassemble that night. By the morning of the 25th the majority of the Regiment had reunited and continued the retirement upon Le Cateau, acting with the 1st Cavalry Brigade. That evening when near Romeries, hopes were raised high by the report that German Cavalry were moving forward to the attack. The whole of the Division turned north eager for a mounted fight, but no enemy were forthcoming, and reluctantly the squadrons withdrew towards Le Cateau.

Darkness fell, and owing to the congestion of infantry and transport on the roads, and the necessity for giving place to slower moving units, it was not till the early hours of the morning that the Headquarters of the Regiment found themselves on the southern outskirts of the town.

On August 26 the memorable battle of Le Cateau was fought. During the greater part of the day Colonel Mullens, with Regimental Headquarters and two Squadrons, acted in conjunction with the 1st Cavalry Brigade, watching the right flank of General Smith-Dorrien's Army.

Retirement continued during the night of the 26th, and on the afternoon of the 27th a portion of the Regiment, with other units of the 2nd Cavalry Brigade, took up a position covering St. Quentin from the north.

Many stragglers of different units had collected in the town, some four hundred men, and all very weary. It was here that Major Bridges found them, and with the aid of a penny whistle and a toy drum raised their enthusiasm and stirred them into life.

9

This little episode of the war has been put into verse by
Sir Henry Newbolt, and is inserted by kind permission :—

"THE TOY BAND"

A SONG OF THE GREAT RETREAT

Dreary lay the long road, dreary lay the town,
  Lights out and never a glint o' moon.
Weary lay the stragglers, half a thousand down,
  Sad sighed the weary big Dragoon :
" Oh ! if I'd a drum here to make them take the road again.
  Oh ! if I'd a fife to wheedle : Come, boys, come !
You that mean to fight it out, wake and take your load again,
  Fall in ! Fall in ! follow the fife and drum ! "

" Hey ! but here's a toy shop, here's a drum for me,
  Penny whistles too, to play the tune !
Half a thousand dead men soon shall hear and see
  We're a band ! " said the weary big Dragoon.
Rubadub ! Rubadub ! Wake and take the road again,
  Wheedle-deedle-deedle-dee ! Come, boys, come !
You that mean to fight it out, wake and take your road again,
  Fall in ! Fall in ! Follow the fife and drum !

Cheerily goes the dark road, cheerily goes the night,
  Cheerily goes the blood to keep the beat.
Half a thousand dead men marching on to fight
  With a little penny drum to lift their feet.
Rubadub ! Rubadub ! Wake and take the road again,
  Tweedle-deedle-deedle-dee ! Come, boys, come !
You that mean to fight it out, wake and take your road again,
  Fall in ! Fall in ! Follow the fife and drum !

As long as there's an Englishman to ask a tale of me,
  As long as I can tell the tale aright,
We'll not forget the penny whistle's Wheedle-deedle-dee !
  And the big Dragoon a-beating down the night.
Rubadub ! Rubadub ! Wake and take the road again,
  Wheedle-deedle-deedle-dee ! Come, boys, come !
You that mean to fight it out, wake and take your load again,
  Fall in ! Fall in ! Follow the fife and drum !

They marched off in good heart, headed by Major Bridges,
who, after accompanying them some way on the road, returned
to the town. The Mayor played up well, and the women of
the town performed prodigies in getting everybody fed.

It may be of interest to readers to be informed that the Author —at the time an Army Chaplain attached to Army Headquarters—passed through St. Quentin during the short time which elapsed between the retirement of the main body of infantry and the arrival of Major Bridges.

He can vouch for the condition of the stragglers in the town. Cut off from their units, wearied by continual day and night marching, fed by the villagers on fruit and wine of the country, they were incapable of pulling themselves together. Persuasion, cajoling, threats of early capture by the on-coming enemy, were all unavailing, the only response to the appeal being a hopeless shake of the head. Men were scattered about the town, propped up against the walls of houses, sleeping on pavements, or lying in gutters, numbed by fatigue and lack of sleep.

It was at such a moment that Major Bridges arrived and received the inspiration of the " penny drums and whistles."

The Author was probably one of very few, if not the only British officer who was afforded opportunity at this particular moment of witnessing this remarkable state of affairs in St. Quentin.

"THE TOY BAND"

The music, by Sir Richard Paget, will be found in Appendix IV. Copies can be obtained from the Publishers, Messrs. J. Curwen & Sons, 24, Berners Street, London, W.1 (Price two shillings), from whom also the setting of the bandscore can be had.

CHAPTER IV

THE TURNING POINT OF THE RETREAT

WHILE this work was being done in St. Quentin, Colonel Mullens, with the main portion of the Regiment, had crossed the Somme at St. Simon to join up with General de Lisle. On the 28th the 2nd Cavalry Brigade was reassembled and moved to Le Plessis, near Guiscard. The Regiment for the first time since the action of Audregnies was reunited and spent the night billeted in farms near Le Plessis.

In the early hours of the 29th, just as the Regiment was falling in on parade, an attack was launched on Le Plessis by the enemy The Brigade moved out to meet the attack, but a general retirement was ordered. Falling back by way of Guiscard, a rearguard action was fought all the way. The enemy being unable to force their way through Guiscard, a fresh attack was launched upon our left, which necessitated a further retirement upon Noyon. During this fighting Lieutenant Sanderson was wounded and taken prisoner, with nineteen other ranks.

The retirement continued through the beautiful Forest of Compiègne, where turf rides and shady trees proved a relief from the hard *pavé* roads and baking sun. A halt was necessary at Compiègne, while the work of the Royal Engineers was covered during the blowing up of the bridge over the Oise. An extra night's march had now to be put in to frustrate an attempt of the enemy to get round the right flank of the Army and cut off our retreat on Paris. Traces of the work of a German Cavalry Brigade were to be found in the remains of a motor transport column, which had been destroyed, and the body of a motor-cyclist despatch rider which was lying by the side of the road pierced with many lance wounds. The arrival of our Cavalry Division appeared to sufficiently scare the enemy, who showed no further intention of trying to get in behind us. During this movement four of the enemy's guns were found by the 19th Hussars, who were attached to us for duty.

Still the retirement continued southwards. The Regiment

passed viâ St. Vaast on the Oise, Senlis, the Forest of Ermonon-ville, near Dammartin, approaching always nearer to Paris.

On September 3 the Regiment was at Gournay, a village on the south bank of the River Marne, and only a few miles east of Paris. September 5 found the Regiment still moving south towards Limoges, some ten miles north of Melun, but on that afternoon a change of direction was ordered. At last we were moving east towards the Germans, who were reported moving south-west.

The following day, September 6, was to be a day of great historical interest. The 2nd Cavalry Brigade was in advance, with the Regiment as advanced guard, and near Pecy, north-west of Provins, the culminating point of the German advance was actually witnessed, Von Kluck's advance cavalry bumping into the Regiment, as it led the Brigade. From that moment our advance began, and the order was issued to push on vigor-ously to the attack in the general direction of La Ferte Gaucher and the Petit Morin.

On September 7, near Montcel, a handful of 9th Lancers, led by their Colonel, David Campbell, and his Adjutant, Captain Reynolds, charged a largely superior force of the 1st Garde Dra-gooner Regiment, the crack German Cavalry of their Garde Corps.

Two days later followed a smart brush with the enemy infantry, who were holding the bridge-head over the Petit Morin at Sablonnières. Lieutenant Jones (13th Hussars), attached to " C " Squadron, was ordered by the Brigadier to charge on to the barricaded bridge with drawn swords.

The first bridge was successfully carried, but the Troop was held up by the barricade on the second one. Meanwhile, " A " Squadron opened an attack down the river bank from the east. The remainder of " C " Squadron with a machine gun, and supported by a squadron of the 18th Hussars, advanced and carried the bridge, which was eventually taken over by the Guards Brigade.

During this operation " B " Squadron, crossing the river over a barricaded bridge held by the enemy, advanced to La Marlière Farm, and finally Basseville. Here Private Thomas was killed, and Lieutenant Gordon-Munro was wounded while carrying a message.

Enemy aeroplanes at this time were very active, and cover in woods had often to be sought.

The advance north continued, the Brigade crossing the River Marne at Chezy-sur-Marne on September 9, heading for the Aisne.

CHAPTER V

THE AISNE

September 13.

THE crossing of the river Aisne at Bourg brought an increase to our casualty list. The approach to Bourg lay by way of two bridges across canals, and lastly the bridge over the river, which however had been destroyed by the enemy. Bourg had been reported by a cavalry patrol " clear of the enemy," but was found by us to be strongly occupied, and a sharp action proved necessary before the town could be entered. Lieutenant Fetherstonhaugh, with a Troop of " B " Squadron, in advance of the Brigade, found the enemy entrenched along the canal bank. " A " Squadron advanced on Villers, where bridges were found to have been blown up, and German infantry were entrenched along the canal here, while both Squadrons came under heavy shell fire. A battery opened fire, while a machine-gun was brought into action at each bridge-head. " C " Squadron was sent to support " B," followed by two Squadrons of the 9th Lancers, which resulted in both bridges being in our hands by the middle of the morning. The enemy driven from their position, Bourg was immediately occupied. While looking for a position for his machine guns Captain FitzGerald was killed, the first officer in the Regiment to fall. Devoted to his guns, as Machine Gun Officer, beloved by all ranks, his death was a great sorrow and loss to the Regiment. During the engagement Corporals Chapman and Savory were killed, Captain Sewell and four other ranks wounded. On the north bank of the river a chase followed after the rear-guard of the enemy.

Continuing the advance during the day we remained in constant action till evening. The Brigade was relieved by the infantry, while we retired to billets at Œuilly, for half a night's rest before another busy day.

14

September 14.

Moving off at 3 a.m. as leading Brigade to the Division, with orders to march on Troyon, we soon came under heavy shell fire at Vendresse. Here the First and Second Armies came up and became heavily engaged with the enemy. The First Army experiencing difficulty in crossing the Aisne, the 2nd Cavalry Brigade was ordered to support the Guards Brigade, and for that purpose was moved up to Soupir. For the next few days, with bad weather, continuous night work, and heavy shelling from the enemy, life was not of the pleasantest. From the 16th to the 19th the Brigade had been filling up a gap between the left of the 2nd and the right of the 3rd Division.

September 19.

This proved to be a red-letter day for " B " and " C " Squadrons. The First Army was in difficulties, and, General de Lisle perceiving that our infantry were being pushed back and forced from their trenches in a position on high ground north of Paissy, orders were received that the Regiment should, if possible, retake the trenches. " B " and " C " Squadrons galloped across an intervening valley of about one and a half miles which led to a very steep hill, thickly wooded, and ended in a sharp " scarp " bordering a plateau. Here the infantry were leaving the hill, and had already fallen back about a thousand yards. Leaving orders to Captain Hornby to dismount the two Squadrons, Major Bridges went forward on foot and reconnoitred. On coming over the top of the rise, he picked up an officer of an infantry regiment, whom he then took forward to view the situation. Here the Germans were seen advancing in fairly large numbers, and some appeared to have got round the right flank. An attack seemed to be developing from our troops on the left. Major Bridges waving to Captain Hornby to come on, the men came up at a sharp double, deploying as they moved up. The Germans were met at some three or four hundred yards' distance, and a hot fire was opened on them, our men still standing up. The Germans took to their heels, whereupon we advanced to within two hundred yards of the Chemin des Dames, where we were ordered to lie down and keep up a sharp fire on the Germans, who were now retreating over the top of the next rise. Major Bridges then went back and found the officer commanding the West Yorkshire Regiment and ordered him to advance his Battalion, which he did. Two of his Companies had been captured, but he mustered some three or four hundred rifles, and soon moved up to where the cavalry were lying.

Led by Major Bridges, the cavalry and infantry moved forward until they reached the original infantry position, which had already been entrenched. This was accomplished practically without loss, while there was a good deal of rifle fire and some shelling. As the cavalry were now lying very exposed, Major Bridges withdrew them another two hundred yards on to some intervening ground where some scooped-out rifle-pits had been made. Shortly after General de Lisle arrived and Major Bridges conferred with him. He was very enthusiastic in his praise of the two Squadrons. Later these Squadrons were withdrawn to rejoin the remainder of the Regiment, which had been occupying a position on a scarp farther to the west, where the Regiment remained in support well into the night. The arrival of a fresh battalion of infantry, the position was considered to be secure. Next day Sir Douglas Haig saw " C " Squadron on parade and congratulated the men on what they had done.

Casualties during these days had been slight in proportion to the work accomplished

About this time the German Emperor afforded some interesting food for thought in the way of an Order to his Army, which had been published the previous month:

" It is my Royal and Imperial Command that you concentrate your energies for the immediate present upon one single purpose, and that is, that you address all your skill and all the valour of my soldiers to exterminate the treacherous little Army of the English, and walk over General French's contemptible little Army.

Headquarters, Aix-la-Chapelle. 19.8.'14.''

At this time the 2nd Cavalry Division, consisting of the 3rd and 5th Cavalry Brigades under the command of General Gough, had been formed, and a Cavalry Corps under the command of General Allenby had been brought into existence. The formation of the Cavalry Corps led to the appointment of Brig.-General de Lisle to command the 1st Cavalry Division, while Lieut.-Colonel Mullens succeeded to the command of the 2nd Cavalry Brigade, the command of the Regiment falling to Major A. Solly-Flood.

CHAPTER VI

FLANDERS—MESSINES

October 12.

THE position of the British front was now changed, the line of the Aisne being handed over to the French, while Sir John French's Army, pivoting on the extreme left of the Aisne line, swung round to take up a flanking position on the right flank of the German Army, necessitating a long march by way of Amiens. This change of front from the Aisne to West Flanders occupied the best part of a week, and on October 12 the Regiment was in front of Bailleul opposite a strong enemy position. The Ypres Salient was to prove the scene of operations for the cavalry for many months to come, and the holding of the salient to cost the British Army dear. As the position of our Army became consolidated and a complete system of entrenchment works extended across the Flanders front, the work of the cavalry became that of mobile infantry, to be called upon in emergency to fill up gaps, cover the movements of infantry as they exchanged positions, and do their allotted term of trench defence. Report said that eight German Cavalry Divisions faced seven French and two English Cavalry Divisions in this section of the front. Lack of maps and dense fog made reconnoitring difficult, continual work of this kind falling to us from the time of our occupation of the district, between Flêtre-Meteren-Steenwerck, along which line we were continually in touch with the enemy. A sharp brush with them came on October 20 round the Bois de Ploegsteert, where the 18th Hussars had been forced to withdraw. In supporting them and the infantry, a nasty situation arose through the enemy working round our rear. Infantry reserves, sent to restore the position with their machine guns, failed and lost their officers. The 9th Lancers, coming up to turn the enemy's flanking movement, became divided through shell fire on the way, but half the Regiment succeeded in stopping the enemy, who, failing to get round the flank, now attacked down the whole line. The position was however maintained till nightfall, when the occupation of Le Gheer by the Somerset Light Infantry in face of very strong opposition restored the line. Captain Hornby and Lieutenant Darley were wounded during this engagement, the former very seriously.

October 28.

After a spell of outpost duty before Messines, the Brigade was ordered to support the Second Corps at Neuve Chapelle. The 2nd Cavalry Brigade was now to find itself supporting the 7th Infantry Brigade, neighbours at Tidworth before the war. The Second Corps was operating in the district around the Lille-La Bassée Road, and after leaving horses at La Coutre, the Regiment proceeded on foot to support the infantry at Richebourg St. Vaast, which was reached on the morning of October 27. The recapture of Neuve Chapelle by the 7th Infantry Brigade was ordered on the following day, the 2nd Cavalry Brigade to co-operate in the attack. The Indian Division, just arrived from India, were also under the command of General McCracken, commanding the 7th Infantry Brigade, and to the Indian troops was entrusted the main attack on the village. This was pushed most vigorously and with great gallantry, but without allowance for the development of the flank attack, with the result that the Indian troops were forced back in the centre and fell back through the line taken up by the cavalry-in-support. This placed the Brigade in the firing line, but owing to the enforced retirement of the infantry, the right flank of the cavalry was left " in the air " and was turned. On the left of the line was the 2nd Cavalry Brigade, and the French continued the line on the right. The turning of our flank brought a fine piece of work by " B " and " C " Squadrons and the 9th Lancers, who were called upon to make the line good, and in spite of the heavy attack made by the enemy and the loss by " C " Squadron of all its officers, the position was maintained. In this severe fighting Captain Oldrey (commanding " C " Squadron) was killed and Lieutenants Jones (attached) and J. Holman were wounded, the latter dying from his wounds two days later.

Captain Oldrey started the War as Regimental Adjutant

and was given command of " C " Squadron in succession to Captain Hornby. Slightly wounded a few days before, he was killed at the head of his squadron while gallantly leading it. A keen and very able soldier, gallant and cool in action, his was a distinct personality whose loss can never be replaced in the Regiment to which he was so devoted.

Lieutenant J. Holman had joined the Regiment two years before the War and had served continuously with " C " Squadron until his death. He was wounded in saving a brother officer, from which wound he died a few days after admission to hospital. Every officer and man was deeply affected by the death of " Little Johnnie," as he was affectionately known to all. Twenty-one N.C.O.'s and men were killed and wounded during the day. After supporting the Second Corps on their part of the line, the Brigade returned to its own sector in front of Messines, with Neuve Eglise as Brigade Headquarters.

October 30 brought us into Messines in support of the 1st Cavalry Brigade, which was being hard pressed. Support was first given when the 1st Brigade was occupying a position on the south-east side of the town. " B " Squadron, joining the 5th Dragoon Guards, was soon driven to take up a position in the middle of the town, as one by one the houses in the first line were blown to pieces by the enemy. " B " and " C " Squadrons now found themselves holding the houses forming the north side of the market-square, while the enemy's snipers kept up a constant fire from the other side of it, one hundred and fifty yards away. Barricades were thrown up at the exits to the village. The enemy rushed up a field gun on a trolley to the barricade on the north side and strongly shelled our position all night. The King's Own Yorkshire Light Infantry and the King's Own Scottish Borderers came up to try to reoccupy the trenches, but were unable to do so. All our guns meanwhile had been withdrawn to Wolverghen, to take up a covering position ; the night was spent in making good our position in readiness for an expected attack in the morning. A line of trenches had been prepared for retirement east of Wolverghem, and owing to troops on our left falling back without notice, and the advance of large masses of the enemy in that direction, retirement to the prepared line became necessary. Assisted by a Squadron of the 18th Hussars and

a Company of King's Own Scottish Borderers, " B " Squadron held
the barricade commanding the exits from the town, while the line
was withdrawn to the new position east of Wolverghem. During
the retirement " B " Squadron lost half a Troop, and a Platoon
of the King's Own Scottish Borderers was wiped out. Casualties
were heavy in the Regiment, Lieutenant S. J. W. Railston (18th
Lancers I.A.) lost his life whilst gallantly trying to save an old
Flemish woman who had wandered between the British and
German firing-lines, and 2nd Lieutenant H. O. Powell, who had
only joined a few days before, being killed on reconnaissance.
Wounded : Captains J. C. M. Kirkwood and A. Wright, Lieutenants D. S. Davison and R. G. Fetherstonhaugh ; forty-one other
ranks being killed and wounded.

The enforced retirement from Messines had now been
necessitated by the reinforcements of the enemy, and their
advance in great numbers, until, owing to the failure to hold
the line complete on our left, our position was threatened from
the rear. In spite of a terrific bombardment from the enemy
and an unfortunate misunderstanding on our own side, the
retirement was nevertheless carried out with good order, well
covered by " B " Squadron. The enemy continued to press
the attack on our new line, part of it south of the Wolverghen-
Messines road being forced, " B " Squadron was ordered to assist
them in regaining the line. Owing to the existence of a long
gap on the right of our position, it was found impossible when
the enemy advanced in strength to hold this line, and a new
one had to be taken up, forming an extension to one already
occupied by the French infantry. The position continued to
be very heavily shelled, and infantry attacks followed one another
in quick succession. The 2nd Cavalry Brigade, reinforced by
the Oxfordshire Hussars attached to the Brigade, now relieved
the 1st Cavalry Brigade and suffered severely from a terrific
fire from the enemy's howitzers, our trenches being blown in
and several men buried alive. During the day Lieutenant
Elmslie, while in command of the machine-gun detachment,
and Lieutenant Ramsay, were killed, Lieutenants Thwaites and
Chance wounded, other ranks losing to the number of thirty-six
killed and wounded. The regimental machine gunners, although
the officer in charge was killed early in the day, fought with
great gallantry under Sergeant Woodland and maintained their
position, covering our left, keeping connection with the French

right, against which the main German attacks were launched. The fire of Sergeant Woodland's gun, which was isolated for twenty-four hours, stopped the advance of a German battalion on two occasions.

He was recommended 'for the Victoria Cross and awarded the Distinguished Conduct Medal for this action.

A long and stubborn fight was put up by Lieutenant Thwaites's party of twelve men, who, being cut off in their trench, repeatedly repulsed the attacks of the enemy. They maintained their position until relieved by the Oxfordshire Yeomanry.

Lieutenant Ramsay was buried in Dranoutre churchyard.

A few days of comparative inaction subsequently followed, while the Brigade was moved from place to place to support different units, and on November 6 we found ourselves again in front of Messines relieving the 1st Cavalry Brigade.

(*Editorial Note.*—It is noted with interest that on the arrival of a Padre, attached to " A " Squadron, the holding of Divine Service is mentioned in the Regimental Diary for the first time during the campaign, followed by a smoking concert !)

CHAPTER VII

YPRES

November 10.

YPRES was visited a few days later, when the Brigade was again on the move; but the town was skirted, signs of heavy bombardment were visible, and the town had already begun to suffer. A visit to the Cloth Hall showed that, though considerably knocked about, the famous frescoes were still to be seen on the walls, pierced in many places by huge shell-holes, while the floor of the building was strewn with debris and piece of beautiful carving. It was the beginning of the end to an historical old building, standing on ground which will always remain hallowed to the memory of the many thousands of Imperial British troops who fell around during the years of struggle for the retention of this important line, the key to our whole position on this sector of the front. Ypres, restored to its former glory, will stand as a visible memorial to those men who fell around it.

November 13.

The next week was spent in marching and counter-marching to support and relieve the 1st Cavalry Brigade in the various positions the Cavalry Division was called upon to hold in the salient. On November 13, supporting Lord Cavan's Division in the wood on the Ypres-Zonnebeke Road, we found the German trenches within fifty yards of our own; in places our advance trenches ran almost into the German position. This wood was in a horrible state, tree-tops being cut off by shells, and from trunk to trunk in front of both positions barbed wire had been slashed, while the undergrowth was entwined with loose rolls of wire. In the many assaults on both sides, men caught in the wire had been shot where they were stranded, strung on the strands from tree to tree. A reconnaissance by Lieutenant

22

Harrison, Commanding " C " Squadron, gave us the information
that part of the German trenches had been vacated, being piled
up with dead, the result of an attack the previous night. His
party had been heavily fired upon from enemy trenches on either
flank, and they were forced to retire. The weather at this
time was intensely cold, the coldest of that winter 1914–15,
snow falling heavily with sharp frost. Owing to this and strain
of overwork, sickness appeared among the Squadrons; a short
rest in billets proved acceptable, and gave opportunity for
repair of boots, which were rotting from continual standing in
snow and mud. Château Herintage, the centre of the Cavalry
Division, provided intense fighting at close quarters, our advance
position, the stable of the Château, and a small trench, being
within twelve yards of those of the enemy. On occupation
this stable proved to have been the scene of hand-to-hand
fighting some considerable time previous, the stalls and men's
rooms above being full of British and German dead, while the
floors were strewn with hand grenades, upon which our party
" skated " on entering in the dark. Fortunately these bore
our weight without explosion, the full relief of which was experienced in the morning when daylight revealed the presence of
a mine placed by the retiring enemy in the centre of the building.
Connection wires had either not been linked up, or had been
displaced, but it was decided to remove this uncongenial stranger
altogether, and mine and bombs were placed where it was hoped
they might still be of service against their constructors.

November 15.

The arrival of a Colonel of the Engineers during the night
led to the construction of a long-shaped loophole round the
corner of the stable. This in the morning was found to command
a view down the German front trench leading from a network
of enemy trenches, interspersed with improvised shelters, and
strongly manned. This proved an admirable target to our
marksmen. A sharpshooter of " A " Squadron, selected for
the work of sniping from this point of vantage, placed no less
than forty-two bulls to his credit during the day. Some time
elapsed before the enemy were convinced that some advantage
had been gained in the command of the position during the
night, but it appeared doubtful that the construction of the

loophole was known to them up to the time of our handing over the trenches to the 3rd Cavalry Brigade at nightfall. The position shortly afterwards being taken over by the French, it was at once decided by them to level the stable to the ground as being untenable. Horses were brought up in rear of the Château, and the Regiment marched back on the night of the 19th to St. Jean Capelle, by way of Ypres, which now showed signs of heavy bombardment. The Regiment was next called upon to occupy trenches vacated by the Oxfordshire Hussars Yeomanry, who had now been attached to the 2nd Cavalry Brigade. This occupation of trenches by us was remarkable as the first occasion on which we were sent up and returned without suffering a single casualty. Heavy snow and frost at this time made fighting difficult, braziers having to be used in the trenches to thaw the machine guns, which were continually freezing. Another joy-ride back to billets on motor-'buses also marked this occasion. Great news too awaited us on return to billets—leave of seventy-two hours to be granted to three officers per regiment to proceed home, the prelude to still better things, when seven days' leave was granted in December to officers and men.

St. Jean Capelle being selected for our winter quarters, stables were constructed, and we settled down to make them as comfortable as circumstances permitted. Hop-poles and felting, procured locally, provided the material for the construction of stables, each Squadron vying with the others to produce the best, while a Riding School was made at Regimental Headquarters, and later a promising " jumping course " was prepared but abandoned on the publication of an order by the Commander-in-Chief that race meetings were prohibited.

December 9.

The General Officer Commanding-in-Chief inspected and addressed the Regiment on December 2, and on the same day Quartermaster-Sergeant Syzling and Squadron-Sergeant-Major Talbot were presented with French medals by the Commander-in-Chief. Two days later the Regiment was reviewed by H.M. the King as part of the 1st Cavalry Division on the Meteren-Flêtre Road. By December 9 the arrival of drafts of officers and men had brought the Regiment up to war establishment in officers, N.C.O.'s, men, and horses.

CHAPTER VIII

1914—1915

THE YPRES SALIENT

" An account of the 4th Royal Irish Dragoon Guards in the Ypres Salient," by MAJOR-GENERAL A. SOLLY-FLOOD, C.M.G., D.S.O., *and re-published by kind permission of the Publishers of " The Ypres Book of Valour."*

THE 4th Royal Irish Dragoon Guards formed part of the advanced guard of cavalry when the British Armies in France were moved from the Aisne back again into Flanders. Up to that time the Regiment had more than its share of fighting.

On August 22, 1914, it had its first brush with the enemy at Soignies near Mons, killing and capturing about thirty Uhlans. In this affair Captain Hornby gained the D.S.O. for being the first British officer to " blood " his sword. From this date on it had many interesting combats, including the so-called charge side by side with the 9th Lancers at Audregnies on August 24, when the Regiment lost about half its effectives and became very split up, the various portions fighting in different parts of the battlefield and not being fully re-united until the 28th at St. Quentin. On this occasion Lieutenant Gallagher had his leg broken and was captured by the enemy. In company with Sergeant Hines of the Band, he escaped from hospital and walked —in spite of the broken leg—many successive nights through the enemy's lines to the coast, got across to England, and reported himself at the War Office. Lieutenant Sir Alfred Hickman was wounded and taken prisoner.

After Audregnies the Regiment reinforced itself frequently on the battlefield by picking up troops and squadrons of other cavalry units which had for the time being lost their own head-quarters, and fought them as part of itself until the latter were discovered. At Le Cateau two squadrons of the 19th Hussars were attached to the Regiment, which was protecting the left flank of the infantry during the battle. It played an important rôle in covering the withdrawal of the infantry from the battlefield, one of the squadrons of the 19th taking on, and most effectively disposing of two squadrons of Uhlans who were audacious enough to follow up too closely. This occurred between Le Cateau and Maretz; afterwards the retirement was continued to Rancourt, which place was reached at about 12 midnight, and had been designated as the rallying-point of the 2nd Cavalry Brigade. Instead of the latter, General Gough's Brigade was there. He expressed his intention of retiring to St. Quentin during the night, and detailed the Composite, 4th Dragoon Guards/19th Hussars Regiment for rear-guard.

St. Quentin was reached about 4 a.m., where the remainder of the 2nd Cavalry Brigade and considerable elements of the Regiment were found to have already arrived, and the latter was re-organized.

St. Quentin is chiefly memorable to the writer because on arrival he was able, with the help of a French interpreter, to take his boots off for the first time since leaving Mons. Having got them off, nothing would induce them to go on again short of slitting them from toe to ankle. A few days later these same boots became the treasured possession of a cyclist orderly.

From St. Quentin the retirement was continued, and the Regiment seemed to be eternally on rear-guard. There were many actions, such as those at Le Petit Plat d'Oie, where Captain Sanderson was wounded and taken prisoner, and outside Noyon, and there were many incidents, some serious and some serio-comic, such as at Guiscard, where the O.C. rear-guard and his horse being blown sky-high by a " coal box," alighting upside down on terra firma, gave themselves a shake, and continued the job on hand. And so on down to Gournay on the Seine.

From here fortune changed, and it had the luck of heading back Von Kluck's advanced guard at Pécy, and was engaged with the enemy more or less seriously via the Petit Morin, near to which stream Lieutenant Gordon-Monro was wounded, to the Marne, and on to the Aisne at the crossing of which, at Bourg, Lieutenant Pat Fitzgerald was killed and Major Sewell wounded. Here it occupied trenches near Paissy, Chavonne, and the Chemin des Dames. Two squadrons executed a counter-attack on foot from the neighbourhood of Paissy, and regained the trenches out of which some of our infantry had been ejected. In October, on its way back into Flanders, it was heavily engaged at many places, such as the Forêt de Nieppe, Le Bisset, Le Gheer where Captain Hornby was badly wounded, as were also Lieutenants Denis Darley and de Warter.

At Ploegstert Wood the enemy broke through the infantry on the right of the Regiment at Le Gheer, and penetrated far behind into the wood. The position was stabilized by the use of two troops which had been held in reserve, and later a squadron of 9th Lancers were sent into the wood to further protect the right flank. The situation stood thus until the arrival of the Somerset Light Infantry the following morning, who retook Le Gheer.

At Neuve Chapelle " C " Squadron lost all its officers, Captain Oldrey and 2nd Lieutenant Holman being killed and Lieutenant Jones badly wounded ; the squadron was, in fact, practically wiped out in the heroic defence of " Gibraltar." Sergeant Sessions here earned great distinction for gallantry in command of the remnants of the squadron. The Regiment also fought at Messines and at Wychaete Crossroads.

The night following the gallant attack by the London Scottish on Messines, the Regiment, which had already one squadron in Messines, was ordered to relieve the 1st Cavalry Brigade which was holding that place.

On arrival, the situation in the little town was found to be most obscure. We were holding the western portion, and there were improvised barricades across all the streets. In the dusk, figures glad in khaki moved about in the Square near the Church, came up to our barricades, and shot into our loopholes, but an order to shoot anyone appearing on the enemy side of any barricade regardless of how dressed soon stopped that, and a method of reinforcing over the garden walls at the back of the houses and a countersign was introduced.

About 4.30 a.m. heavy firing was heard from the direction of Wychaete and the windmill on the Wychaete Road. On visiting our squadron near the windmill it was found to be heavily engaged : in a barn they were holding, our men and the enemy were using alternate loopholes, and if you stood opposite the wrong one you got shot in the leg, at the same time columns of heavy infantry could be seen approaching the Wychaete Road, and information came in that our troops had been driven out of Wychaete Village.

The local situation was quickly restored, the enemy were ejected from the barn, and a squadron of 18th Hussars which had been in reserve advanced as far as the windmill, driving back considerable numbers of the enemy, who were approaching the Wolverghem Road with a view to cutting off Messines.

At about 7 a.m. the enemy renewed his attack on the windmill in great numbers, and eventually, having turned the flank of the 18th Hussars, drove them back over the Wolverghem Road. The situation was very serious, but the 18th Hussars rallied, a troop of the 4th Dragoon Guards was withdrawn from the right in Messines Village and the machine gun of the Regiment was brought into action to support the counter-attack which was launched with these few devoted officers and men. By 9 a.m. the situation was again restored, though at considerable cost, and once more we occupied the windmill and the left flank was secured and the Wolverghem Road once more open.

There were no supports or reserves of any sort left in that little garrison.

A message was sent back to Brigade-Headquarters asking for reinforcements, and the answer came back that there were none, and further that if we could not maintain our position without them, we were to retire to the next position, which was occupied by London Scottish and 9th Lancers, and that the withdrawal would be covered by artillery. There was nothing for it but to vacate the town which had cost us so dear to hold. Railston and Powell had been killed, Kirkwood, Wright, Davison and Fetherstonhaugh wounded.

The withdrawal was carried out without mishap other than that our guns mistook us for the enemy, and the officer conducting the retirement had a narrow shave of emulating Absalom, being caught by his scarf in a barbed wire fence, an enemy machine gun—late as they were in following up—made a target of him. Their shooting, however, was poor.

It was interesting to learn from a captured German officer that he could not believe Messines had been held for so long by cavalry. The Germans imagined that it was held by a picked corps of machine-gunners. The number of machine guns with British units were limited to two in those days, so we may take it that the rifle shooting of the cavalry was only excelled by the manipulation of their bolts.

After the fall of Messines the enemy continued to press their attack in numbers, and covered it with the heaviest concentration of artillery yet experienced.

The Regiment occupied a line of detached trenches on the right of the French, with whom we joined up at Wychaete Crossroads. This was a vital spot, and the machine-gun detachment was told off to cover it.

Intense artillery fire was maintained on our positions from early morning, followed up at intervals by infantry assaults. The French on our left were shelled out of their trenches.

Our trenches were blown in and many officers and men buried, but our machine guns, under Sergeant Woodland, held, the officer was killed, and a troop of "B" Squadron, under Lieutenant Thwaites, despite many casualties, also held. The enemy failed to get the crossroads.

With the Queen's Own Oxfordshire Hussars, which regiment was sent up during the day and had been held in support, we all went forward in the dusk of evening to eject the enemy who were in portions of our shattered trenches, and in this manner relieved our machine-gun detachment and the remains of Thwaites's gallant troop, many of whom had to be dug out.

We lost Elmslie and Ramsay killed, and Thwaites and Chance were wounded.

After its last of many dips into the Messines Sector the Regiment was promised forty-eight hours' rest, and was moved on November 11 back to Meteren in the pouring wet, its last elements getting into billets about 10 p.m.

By 1 a.m. the same night we were on the march again, and in the grey dawn of the early morning we found ourselves marching through Ypres in thick snow.

The town was left by the Menin Gate, and our orders were to bivouac and make ourselves comfortable in the grounds of Potijze Château, a farm and a small wood on the left of the Menin Road. There the Regiment stayed and shared such cover as there was with some French Hussars until the evening of the 13th, when it was ordered to relieve the London Scottish in Zillebeke Woods. The relief was not an easy one, for, to add to the difficulties of the weather—a regular downpour of sleet having set in—darkness came on. French troops and British troops, including field and heavy artillery, were marching in all directions. They took up all the roads and tracks, and got stuck in the ditches which were full to overflowing. The guides of the London Scottish, whom we were relieving, miscarried. We however got into our places in the front line trenches in Zillebeke Woods by about midnight

13th/14th. The enemy's trenches were at a distance varying from twenty to fifty yards.

The wood was in a horrible state, many trees were cut down by shells, and a mass of branches and strands of barbed wire separated the opposing trenches. In the many assaults, on both sides, men caught in the wire had been shot, and their bodies were left suspended on the wire, which was strung from tree to tree.

To make matters worse, the weather at the time was intensely cold, the coldest part of the winter of 1914–15, heavy falls of snow alternating with sharp frosts. Fighting was continuous, cooking of food or drying of boots impossible, and the men were too wet and cold to sleep.

Much useful work was done by patrols, who crawled at night through the debris and reconnoitred the enemy's lines. Sergeant Thomas of " C " Squadron on the night of the 13th penetrated into the German trenches, a portion of which had been abandoned, and found them piled with dead. He returned with this and other valuable information, also with sufficient pairs of boots, taken from the freshly killed Germans, to equip his troop. There was considerable good-humoured jealousy expressed in forcible language by the men according as the boots, when they were distributed and fell to their share, were still warm and pliable from their late wearer or were cold and stiff from a long dead enemy. This was our first reinforcement in footwear since leaving England.

The Regiment was relieved about midnight of the 15th/16th, and moved back into billets at Brielen.

On the 17th we were once more in the front line on the right of the Menin Road at Château Heritage.

A humorous incident took place. Brigade H.Q.'s were at Hooge Château, and on the way up to the line the C.O. reported there. After receiving instructions, as he was leaving the Brigade-Major said to him, " The Germans have been throwing hand bombs. You'll find a box of bombs in the Conservatory at the Château."

That was the first we had heard of bombs and certainly never dreamt of having to use them. However, nothing daunted we went on and searched for the " Conservatory." It was snowing " ink," as the expression then went, and eventually we found a place that in the grim darkness looked for all the world like the ribs of a crinoline, but as one walked about on broken glass we knew it must have been a conservatory at one time. Sure enough behind the remains of the door we found a ration biscuit-tin full of what we later got to learn were " Plum and Apple " bombs. An R.E. officer who was in charge of them explained that these were the things to which the Brigade-Major had referred. The difficulty was to find some one in the Regiment who would undertake their manipulation, as no one had been trained in their use. Eventually a subaltern (Gallaher, who had recovered from his wound and had rejoined) volunteered for the job, on the strength of being the last to attend a Pioneer Course at Chatham. The R.E. officer explained amid the darkness that all that was necessary was to strike a match, light the fuse, and throw the bomb. It was pointed out to him that in the Army the custom was to demonstrate after giving an explanation. He said that he had no time to demonstrate, and asked for a few minutes' grace in order to get away. The remainder of the story is best told in Gallaher's own words :

" Before going he (the R.E. officer) said he would like to point out that these bombs were made behind the line, had been brought up in an ammunition wagon, and subjected to a certain amount of jolting, which might cause the powder to drop out of the fuse in which case the bomb would be practically instantaneous ! As soon as he had gone I found that I could not throw the bombs from the trench, which was only five or six yards from the Germans' line, owing to an old hedge being in the way and also because the trench was too narrow. I therefore got up into the doorway of the stable, which was at right angles to the trench, struck a match, and threw the first bomb successfully. I think the reason why the Germans did not fire was they were so surprised at a match being struck within five yards of their line ! On attempting to light the second bomb, I was greeted with a fusillade of fire. I threw several more, and eventually, due to cold—as you will remember the ground was covered with snow— or from fear, I fell from the doorway into our own trench with the bomb in my hand, but had the luck to hurl it out just before it would have exploded amongst the men in the trench. I was cursed by everybody, and told to give it up, and eventually we all settled down into our places."

The stable of the Château, and a small trench running through it, was within, at farthest, twelve yards of the enemy's trenches.

The stable had been the scene of heavy hand-to-hand fighting a short time previous, the floors were littered with hand grenades, the stalls and men's room above were full of British and German dead, and the smell was overpowering, but it was impossible to remove the bodies.

The Troop of " A " Squadron occupying the stable made a narrow loophole which commanded a view down the enemy's front trench and a view of his trench system for some distance. One selected marksman alone accounted for forty-two Germans from this point.

Some days after the Regiment had been relieved from this position, the stable was found to be untenable owing to its state, and to the terrific trench-mortar bombardment directed on it. It was abandoned and levelled to the ground. It was here that we were introduced to trench-mortar bombs—which we christened the " Silent Sausage," and which felled buildings and trees and filled in our miserable trenches. One officer sent word back to say " They are throwing Oat Sacks at us," and set to work to shoot them in the air with a rifle, but was eventually made to desist by his infuriated squadron leader.

Beyond minor attacks, counter-attacks, small breakages in the neighbouring line, which we helped to regain, in one instance having to get up for the purpose all our squadron cooks, transport men and other details from the wagon line, as no other reinforcements were available, all of which events followed each other with surprising swiftness, and appeals for artillery support which was never forthcoming (guns being limited to about four rounds per diem), nothing further happened of outstanding note during our occupation of this savoury spot.

Being relieved on the night of 19th/20th, we picked up our horses at Hooge Château, and the C.O., who was the last to come away, had his horse badly wounded by shrapnel. This was the second time this horse had been badly wounded, it being the same horse which temporarily aped an aeroplane with the assistance of a German " coal box " at Guiscarde ; however, with unlimited care and the aid of a devoted second servant, the faithful animal's life was saved. He lived to win several jumping prizes in Germany in 1919, and his master owns him still. Despite his age, he still gives a good feel over a country not less than one day a week. He will be remembered in the Regiment as being at one time Sergeant Pettitt's horse, No. B. 176.

The Regiment went back to St. Jean Cappelle, and was left in rest for a period.

With the exception that the 4th Dragoon Guards took their turn with other cavalry regiments to go up into the Salient as a working-party for about a week at a time, it took no further part in the defence of Ypres until 1915, in February of which year it had a spell in front-line trenches, and on relief billets in the Reformatory on the Menin Road, which at that time had not become such an unhealthy spot as it did a few months later.

Again early in March it was in front of Zillebeke. But on neither of these occasions did anything of great note happen, beyond taking a hand at sapping, and showing its prowess at sniping, which latter amusement produced furious bombardments from the Boche, which on one occasion knocked out the machine-gun detachment and cut the gun in two.

On April 22, 1915, the 4th Dragoon Guards were in billets round Meteren. On that evening great aeroplane activity and hostile gun fire were noticed in the Salient, and it was hardly a surprise when the 2nd Cavalry Brigade were turned out at 2 a.m. Commanding Officers were informed that the Boche had gassed the French in front of Boesinghe. This was the first gas attack, and there were many conjectures as to how the gas had been employed—pipes, tunnelling, etc., being amongst the suggestions —a gas cloud was not guessed at.

We moved up to Poperinghe, and began to see the first effect of gas.

The 4th Dragoon Guards and 18th Hussars were to dig themselves in, in front of Elverdinghe—behind the French on the Canal, and in front of the French reserve line.

The difficulties of combined operations were instantly apparent, our communications through the 2nd line of French being difficult. This was got over by putting a picket of 9th Lancers (in reserve) on the road.

Elverdinghe was being heavily shelled, and as the Regiment moved up on foot it met with casualties, Lieutenant Brown and eight men being killed by one shell which obliterated them, 2nd Lieutenants Rubie and Honey also were wounded.

The Regiment was shortly relieved, and after holding some reserve trenches at the junction of the French and Belgian lines, was withdrawn on April 26.

The heroic fight of the Canadians at St. Julien had been pro-

D

ceeding on our right, but owing to being heavily engaged ourselves we were powerless to help.

From the 6th to the 8th May, 1915, the Regiment was employed digging a new line of trenches on the canal just north of Ypres. Work was done by night, the sky being lit by the flames from the burning city. Each morning before dawn the Regiment marched back to bivouac near Vlamertinghe. All roads and tracks were subjected to intermittent bursts of shrapnel fire, and on the night of the 7th, Lieutenant Butler and twenty-two men were wounded.

On the 8th the Regiment made a welcome move back to billets in Meteren, only to be turned out at 2.30 the next morning and rushed back to Ypres. Horses were again left at Vlamertinghe, and the rest of the march to reserve trenches at Potijze made on foot. At 8 p.m. orders came to reinforce infantry holding front line on the Zonnebeke Road. The exact position of the trenches was not known, and the C.O., on pressing for more definite orders, was told to march up the Zonnebeke Road till he met a staff-officer who would direct him.

About 11 p.m. the Regiment started off in column of route, and no staff-officer being found, was halted near Valorenhoek, the C.O., Adjutant and leading squadron-leader (De Wiart) going on up the road. Nothing could be seen of our troops or of any sort of defence on the road. It was very dark, and there was no indication of the nearness of the enemy till they challenged and opened heavy fire at what seemed only a few yards' range.

The Headquarter party dropped on the road, only De Wiart being hit. The Adjutant probably did the right thing by shouting and firing his revolver as soon as he could get it clear of coat and waterproof. No doubt the Germans were equally frightened, for the firing stopped and, thinking it over now, it seems probable that they bolted. But at the time this hardly seemed probable of any of the party, who made the best of their way back to the Regiment.

The Adjutant describes it himself as follows :

" After we got into the German lines, and they had opened fire at two or three yards' range and shot De Wiart's arm off, I threw myself on my face in the road and emptied my revolver into the group. In trying to reload I lost all my ammunition in the dark, so threw my empty revolver at them. I then seized the orderly's rifle, only to find that it was not loaded. I then

lost my head, and took to my heels down the road followed by
some one, who in the dark I thought was a Boche. I well remember
falling over dead men, shell-holes and other obstructions in the
road. I was wearing one of those long Italian cloaks which had
been issued, which came to my toes like a sheet with a hole in
it. Every time I trod on it I would turn over like a rabbit.
Several times in running I tried to tear this cloak off but was
unsuccessful. I must have run fast as the man behind me never
overtook me, only gaining a few yards at the various times I
fell. When I looked round the man following me always appeared
in the dark to have a bayonet in his hand. I think now he was
only the orderly, but I have never discovered who he was, as I
easily outpaced him, although I am not a runner."

De Wiart was in great pain and holding his left arm which
was badly shattered by two rifle bullets, and retired with the
C.O. on all fours along the ditch, expecting to see Germans on
the road above them at any minute !

The staff-officer, a very tired and very young one, had by now
appeared, and as it was obvious that there were no defences on
the road or immediately to the right of it, the Regiment spent
the remaining hours of darkness digging against time.

It was a very bad line but better than nothing, and when
the Germans again attacked at dawn they were held.

Movement of any sort during the day was out of the question,
as the position was under direct observation, and within about
two hundred yards of the Germans.

The ration carriers moving up in the grey dawn found themselves under heavy fire with no obvious place to go. Lieutenant
Gibb, who had been our Padre at Tidworth—beloved by all
ranks—and who had joined us shortly before as a fighting soldier,
came to their help, but was shot and blinded as he was getting
them under cover. He and other wounded crawled or were
dragged into shell-holes, where they lay through that long day.

Casualties among squadrons were not very heavy considering
the strength of the attack and the bad siteing of our unfinished
position, but every runner who attempted to move between Regimental Headquarters and the Squadrons was hit.

The Regiment was relieved at midnight by a Battalion of the
East Surrey Regiment, and marched back through the smouldering
City of Ypres to the Goldfish Château, which was reached about
2 a.m. on the 11th.

Rest till the evening of the 12th, when the 2nd Cavalry Brigade occupied front-line trenches just south of Wieltje, the 9th Lancers and the 18th Hussars in the front line, the Regiment in close support. The short hours of darkness were spent in improving the line, and dawn of May 13 broke with a terrific enemy bombardment. This was the herald of successive attacks which continued through the day.

The Regiment, though nominally in support, was in fire action continuously, protecting the right flank of the Brigade, which was threatened from the direction of the Zonnebeke Road, where the 1st Cavalry Brigade were hard-pressed.

Casualties were very heavy, both Commanding-Officer and Adjutant being wounded, the latter very severely. This was the second time both these officers had been wounded.

On May 23, 1915, the Regiment, having been lent to the 9th Cavalry Brigade, had been in the trenches for about ten days in the neighbourhood of St. Julien, Bellewaarde Lake, etc., with its Headquarters at Hooge Château. That night, however, it was relieved by its own Brigade, the 2nd Cavalry Brigade, and was sent into the ramparts at Ypres in reserve, where it arrived about 1 a.m. on the 24th.

About 2.30 a.m. every one was awakened by a terrific Boche bombardment, and at about 3.30 a.m. a sickly smell assailed our nostrils which we knew to be GAS.

The Regiment was then ordered out of their casemates, which had become a death trap, and was drawn up in the open under cover of the ramparts ; we put on gas masks (cotton-wool and muslin : these things resembled nothing so much as what we older folk would remember was the fashion among ladies in the latter part of the last century, called a dress improver) and awaited orders.

Great confusion was reported from the Menin Gate, and the O.C. Regiment posted a troop to collect all stragglers and line them up in the trenches on the ramparts. None were allowed to pass, and some thousands were collected and marshalled.

About 4 a.m. news was received that the 2nd Cavalry Brigade was in difficulties, and that the Regiment was to move up in support. Lieutenant O'Donnell with his troop was sent to get touch with the 9th Lancers, who were in Zouave Wood, and to report. This he did, though badly wounded in the process— no mean performance, a distance of some two thousand yards through a gas-laden heavily shelled zone.

Exit was made through the Lille Gate, and the Regiment moved in troop columns to the railway cutting just short of the level-crossing at Hell Fire Corner, sustaining a few casualties on the way.

At about 6.30 a.m. the G.O.C. 9th Cavalry Brigade sent for the O.C. 4th Dragoon Guards and said that reliable information had been received that the G.H.Q. line, north of the Menin Road, had been captured by the enemy. Despite all protest no time could be permitted for reconnaissance, and the 4th Dragoon Guards were to proceed at once and recapture the line. The O.C. 4th Dragoon Guards ordered troop columns once more, and led his regiment, by bounds wide of and over the " cursed " level-crossing and past the Reformatory, to the attack. Going some distance in advance himself, he discovered that the G.H.Q. line, instead of having been captured, was crammed with British troops, leaving no room for his regiment to get cover in. He ordered the Regiment to halt where it was short of the G.H.Q. line and take cover in shell-holes and folds of the ground, eventually withdrawing it by driblets to the railway cutting once more. The shell fire had been very heavy, and this operation lost the Regiment about half its effectives.

Shortly after getting back to the railway cutting, the remnants of some reinforcements which had been waiting in Vlamertinghe Camp reported themselves. Remnants in truth : they had started three officers and about sixty men, there arrived two officers and thirty-seven men, one officer and several men wounded among them, one officer and twenty-three having been killed or wounded on the way up, one officer had been blown to pieces, no trace ever having been found of him.

The Regiment was now re-organized, and despite the hard time it had been through, and despite the fact that casualties continued to occur, the spirit of all ranks was splendid. The men re-adjusted their gas protectors, and awaited further orders, under heavy fire both of H.E. and lachrymatory shell, freely interspersed with shrapnel.

The only thing that irked them was inactivity and the impossibility of getting to grips with the " stinking " Boche.

About midday an infantry counter-attack began to develop, and, despite representations made by the O.C. 4th Dragoon Guards, it was pushed on. Those participating were troops new to the country—Territorials from Cheshire and Lancashire—and their baptism of fire was very severe. The Cheshires being mowed down by shell fire, melted away and effected nothing.

As this counter-attack had failed, the O.C. 4th Dragoon Guards made up a composite squadron with the reinforcements, and at about 4 p.m. sent it to occupy Bruree cross roads, so as to fill the gap between O'Donnell's troop in Zouave Wood and the G.H.Q. line north of the Menin Road. This operation was carried out successfully by Lieutenant Darley, and they got the only opportunity afforded the Regiment of punishing the Boche, which they did most effectually, considerable elements of the latter having, as the day wore on, summoned up courage to follow up their own gas and had penetrated the British position with a view to cutting off Zouave Wood.

The remainder of the Regiment was formed into one weak Squadron and stayed in reserve, ready to reinforce in any direction.

The situation did not change up to midnight 24th/25th, at which time we were relieved by elements of the 1st Cavalry Division. Waiting on tenterhooks was not a pleasant occupation, there were continued casualties from shell fire, the weather was very hot and breathless, and the enemy's lachrymatory shells were most unpleasant.

The day had cost us dear : two officers had been killed, four had been wounded, of whom one subsequently died, and one had his knee put out ; the casualties in other ranks were heavy in proportion.

It was a very depleted regiment, consisting of exhausted, hungry and thirsty remnants, that was formed up and taken back to Vlamertinghe Camp in the early hours of the 25th, thus severing the connection of the Regiment with the Ypres Salient, except for the working-parties which it continued to find—half the Regiment at a time—up to the time when it marched from Bollezeele to take part in the Battle of Loos.

No attempt has been made in this brief account of the doings of the Regiment in the earlier days of the war to gauge accurately the casualties suffered, but some idea can be formed from the Officer casualties which have been mentioned in this account of the doings of the Regiment, and from the fact that between the date of landing in France and January 1, 1915, there had been on the regimental books the names of sufficient officers and men to form more than three complete regiments.

CHAPTER IX

1915

YPRES. TRENCH WARFARE

THE New Year found us settled down to a life of training in winter quarters in the vicinity of Bailleul, the different Squadrons and Regimental Headquarters being billeted in farms around St. Jean Capelle, Major Solly-Flood, D.S.O., Commanding, with Major Sewell, Second-in-Command, and Captain Aylmer, Adjutant. The first week of the year was marked by an unofficial visit of H.R.H. the Prince of Wales, who while motoring past joined in a first-rate run with the 2nd Cavalry Brigade beagles, and after hounds had been taken home, took tea at Regimental Headquarters. The Prince showed interest in the hounds, and expressed the hope that he might again hunt with them. These beagles had just arrived from England.

The next few weeks were spent in training, musketry being made a special feature of, through the building of a rifle range at the Trappist Monastery on the Mont des Cats.

The end of February saw a return to the trenches, the 2nd Cavalry Brigade being thrown in for ten days in relief of the infantry. On relief from the trenches, billets were provided in the Reformatory outside Ypres, on the Ypres-Menin Road, where hot baths and a clean outfit of clothing were found. Except for the attention of the enemy's guns, it was generally agreed that a Boys' Reformatory was not such a bad place as sometimes believed. Cubicle baths had their dangers, for freedom from them after the door had closed behind one was only to be gained from without—an awkward predicament in the case of a sudden " turn out." Clothing was subjected to a most thorough boiling and fumigating process, and clean once more—for the moment—we returned to duty in the muddy

39

trenches, later to undergo a second and third process of cleansing, a provision on the part of the R.A.M.C. much appreciated by all ranks.

At this time the Machine Gun Section under Lieutenant Aizlewood was called upon to do continuous duty with the 1st and 2nd Cavalry Brigades.

The first week in March brought a return to the front line, and occupation of trenches in front of Zillebeke, where a network of trenches ran almost from our own lines to those of the Germans. Sapping at night actually opened up a German trench, and the close proximity of the enemy's cook-house offered a tempting target of dixies, with an occasional running shot at the cooks. French gunners placed just behind our line kept up an incessant point-blank bombardment of the German trenches, skimming our parapet, which admitted of no liberty of action either in front or rear, and kept us down flat in two feet of mud. The enemy retaliated by a furious bombardment of our line, and the machine-gun entrenchment of " B " Squadron was knocked out, the gun being cut in two.

A return to billets at Meteren brought little rest to men or horses, a series of turn-outs and marches following one another in support of the infantry during the progress of the battle of Neuve Chapelle between March 10–15. Heavy bombardment of Messines took place simultaneously, while an attack was launched by the enemy on St. Eloi, the counter-attack by the cavalry proving highly successful. A diversion from fighting came on March 17 (St. Patrick's Day), when part of the Regimental band, consisting of eight instrumentalists, gave the accustomed concert. At this time Captain McGillicuddy left the Regiment to take up the duties of assistant instructor at the Machine Gun School at St. Omer. Major Hunter at this time had come out from England and taken over command of the Regiment.

April 19.

Captain A. Carton de Wiart rejoined the Regiment after being seconded for service under the Colonial Office against the Mullah in Somaliland. The weather, which had been bright and sharp with frosts, now broke, and storms of rain and snow with hail and thunder made " going " heavy and swamped the trenches. The break brought the change from winter to spring, and by April 19 hot weather seemed to have set in. A system of regular provision of baths at Flêtre had been much appreciated for the past month, and the health of all ranks was excellent.

The capture of Hill 60 improved our front line about this time, but our next effort was in the direction of Yser, where the Brigade attacked the Germans along the canal line, but little was effected and the Brigade was back in billets by April 20. Two days later the Second Battle of Ypres started, and was to be specially marked by the use of poisonous gases by the enemy. The Brigade was ordered up to support the French and Canadians, who were getting badly mauled around St. Julien, where they had come up against the main German attack, and found the air poisoned with gas fumes. French and Canadians were to be found lying insensible along the roadside, and during the first effects of this method of warfare there was no provision for treatment. Orders were immediately published for the treatment and prevention of effect of fumes: the application of a wet handkerchief to the nose proved but a primitive method of prevention, and soon gave way to gas masks and a more effective system. The effect of these gas fumes was soon to be extended to our horse lines behind Ypres, and the country for a depth of some miles behind the front line was affected. While taking up a position north of Elverdinghe, Lieutenant Brown was killed. Lieutenant Brown had previously served with the Indian Army and had endeared himself to the Regiment while serving with it. The destruction of " B " Squadron would have been complete but for the fact that the enemy's shells fell into soft black mud, in a meadow through which the Squadron was advancing on foot. Meanwhile the Canadians had held on to St. Julien, and the arrival of the 18th French Army Corps relieved the situation. The Germans next pushed across the Yser Canal, occupying the position lately ours, but a counter-attack recovered it for us.

Indian cavalry also arrived in support. The Cavalry Division was constantly broken up during the progress of this Second Battle, its Brigades being thrown in to fill up gaps along the line as required. On return to billets on May 7, Lieutenant Honey was wounded. Two days later the Regiment was on its way to Potighe to take over a position vacated by the infantry. Very heavily shelled while taking up position along Zonnebeke Road, and, owing to defective Staff work on the part of the outgoing Brigade, the Zonnebeke Road was left unheld, and a German patrol passing the front line fired upon our Headquarter party proceeding to take over line, Captain de Wiart being wounded. It was found impossible to take over trenches before 2 a.m., while the ammunition party were forced to make their way into the front line after dawn. The close proximity of the German machine guns brought a heavy fire at twenty yards range; seven men of the party were killed, Lieutenant Gibb being wounded while directing the remainder into the half-dug trenches. Relief followed next day, having to be carried out under very heavy rifle fire, causing many casualties. A return to Ypres found the town in flames, but shelter for men was forthcoming in the undemolished part of the town, while horses were sent back to billets at Meteren.

May 13.

The Regiment was now called upon to find three hundred rifles, if necessary at the cost of Echelon " B " being rendered immobile.

During heavy bombardment Major Sewell and Captain Gallaher were wounded.

Lance-Corporal Smith, who carried despatches between 2nd and 9th Cavalry Brigades with great gallantry, was specially mentioned by the General Officer Commanding 9th Cavalry Brigade, and recommended for the D.C.M. Lieut.-General the Hon. Sir Julian Byng and the General Officer Commanding 9th Cavalry Brigade sent messages of approval of the work of the Regiment.

Considerable changes took place in the Regiment at this time. Lieutenants Chance and Cattley, with fifty-three other ranks, rejoined the Regiment, while Lieutenants Williams and Digby with a draft of men and horses arrived for the first time.

Opportunity was taken of a rest in billets at Wormhouldt for a Memorial Service, which was held on June 6.

Field-Marshal Sir John French inspected the 2nd Cavalry Brigade and congratulated each Regiment on its good work during the previous heavy fighting.

August.

Squadron and regimental training occupied the next month, while a move was made from the billets round Wormhouldt to Bolleezele. During this period of training, one Squadron per Regiment in the Brigade supplied trench-digging parties for the line of defence round Vlamertinghe. At the conclusion of the first year of war the following officers, other ranks, and horses, which came out in 1914, were serving with the Regiment :

	Officers.	Other Ranks.	Horses.
Regimental Headquarters .	3	23	13
Echelon " B " . . .	1	16	12
Machine Gun Section . .	0	18	26
" A " Squadron . . .	0	33	0
" B " Squadron . . .	1	40	37
" C " Squadron . . .	1	34	37
Total	6	164	125

The close of the first year of war found the cavalry still in the Ypres Salient, in occupation of billets near by those occupied after the Army had swung round from the line of the Aisne to the western line of defence in Belgium. From Mons to Ypres viâ Paris, with a month of retreat before the enemy, followed by an advance against the enemy to the Aisne, and terminating in trench-warfare in the Ypres Salient, had been the work of the year.

September.

The following month of September was ushered in by an unfortunate accidental explosion of gun-cotton during a demonstration in bombing, Major Sewell, Lieutenant Chapin, 2nd Lieutenant Lovett and ten other ranks being injured. Trench-digging, training, sports and music occupied most of this time —a cavalry band playing in the market-square at Esquelbecq. Half the Regiment at a time was occupied in building trenches at Vlamertinghe, for which the following appreciation was received from the General Officer Commanding Sixth Army Corps.

" I hope you will express to your Division the gratitude of the 6th Corps for the very great assistance they have rendered to them. It is not only the good solid work that they have done but also the high example they have set. Their unselfish devotion to the performance of what well might have been regarded as a duty which was outside their rôle, has won the admiration of us all. Please express to all ranks our most sincere and heartfelt thanks."

(Signed) J. L. KEIR,

Lieut.-General, Commanding Sixth Corps.

5.9.'15.

Major Sewell rejoined the Regiment on recovery from the effects of the explosion accident. Lieutenant J. C. M. Kirkwood, who, since being wounded at Messines whilst serving with the Regiment, had been attached to the 1st Life Guards, seeing service in Russia, now rejoined the Regiment.

The middle of September brought a move from billets in support of Sir H. Rawlinson's Division at Vandicourt, necessitating a march viâ Fontaine-Nedon-Anettes.

Flags were introduced to be carried by the cavalry when doing dismounted work, for the guidance of the artillery. The regimental establishment of machine-guns was increased from two to four guns.

At this time the work of clearing the battlefields and filling in trenches was shared by the Cavalry Divisions.

The extension of seventy-two hours' leave in England to seven days marked the close of the last quarter of the year. The arrival of reinforcements from home led to the posting of 2nd Lieutenant R. A. Radclyffe and thirteen men to "A" Squadron, thirty N.C.O.s and men to "B" Squadron, 2nd Lieutenant C. G. Bernards-Bryan and thirty N.C.O.s and men to "C" Squadron. Colonel Solly-Flood's appointment to command the 35th Infantry Brigade soon followed his appointment to command the Regiment. Major H. S. Sewell, D.S.O., assumed command of the Regiment on his return from sick leave on November 6.

The new Commanding Officer was decorated by the French Government at this time with the Croix de Chevalier de Légion d'Honneur (Fifth Class), and the Croix de Guerre was handed to Sergeant A. J. Tilney by H.R.H. the Duke of Connaught.

Training occupied the remaining months of the year, while the Regiment was billeted round Maresville.

The end of December brought return to trench work, a Brigade Battalion being formed to assist the First Army.

CHAPTER X

1916

ROLL OF OFFICERS

REGIMENTAL HEADQUARTERS STAFF

Lieut.-Colonel H. S. Sewell, D.S.O., Commanding.
Lieutenant R. J. F. Chance, Adjutant.
Captain A. Gallaher, Intelligence Officer.
2nd Lieutenant D. G. Williams, Signalling Officer.
Lieutenant J. A. Aizlewood, Machine Gun Officer.
2nd Lieutenant G. Dent, Machine Gun Officer.
Lieutenant F. A. Dunham, Quartermaster.

" A " SQUADRON

Captain E. M. Dorman.
Captain H. S. Hodgkin, D.S.O.
Lieutenant H. de G. Warter.
Lieutenant L. F. Marson.
2nd Lieutenant J. B. P. Fitz-Gerald.
2nd Lieutenant L. E. McNeill.
2nd Lieutenant R. A. Radclyffe.
2nd Lieutenant L. E. Misa.

" B " SQUADRON

Captain A. Wright.
Captain R. G. Fetherstonhaugh.
Captain R. J. L. Ogilby.
2nd Lieutenant W. F. Heron.
2nd Lieutenant J. B. Wickham.
2nd Lieutenant G. A. Cattley.
2nd Lieutenant A. M. Odling.

" C " SQUADRON

Captain D. G. F. Darley.
Captain J. C. M. Kirkwood.
Lieutenant C. F. Farley.
Lieutenant T. W. Greenhill.
2nd Lieutenant M. O'Donnell.
2nd Lieutenant C. H. Pillman.
2nd Lieutenant C. G. Bernards-Bryan.
2nd Lieutenant A. P. Williams.

45

WHILE the dismounted Battalion assisted the First Army, the Regimental Headquarters and horses were withdrawn to the Boulogne area, being billeted in and around Longvillers.

The dissolution of the Cavalry Corps came early in the year, bringing the following message from the Corps Commander, Lieut.-General the Hon. C. E. Bingham, C.V.O., C.B. :

> "The Corps Commander wishes to place on record his appreciation of the help and assistance he has received from the Corps Staff and the close co-operation that exists between it and the several Divisions and Brigades. His thanks are due to the splendid Batteries and Regiments which he had the honour to command. The Cavalry Corps having been dissolved, it only remains for the Commander with a very heavy heart to wish all—good luck and God-speed."

The Regiment was employed in February holding the Hohenzollern Redoubt. The trenches were close to the enemy, and there was considerable bombing and mining activity. Lieutenant T. W. Greenhill was killed by a trench mortar. He had served for two years and three months in " C " Squadron, and was mentioned in despatches.

The Machine Gun Corps (Cavalry) was formed at this stage, Lieutenants Aizlewood and Dent with the Machine Gun Section were transferred to the 2nd Machine Gun Squadron.

A lamentable accident, caused by the premature bursting of a hand-grenade, killed the Regimental Bomb and Pioneer Officer, Lieutenant W. F. Heron, and wounded Corporal Wheatley and Private Rearden. Lieutenant Heron had served since April, 1915, with the Regiment with distinction, being mentioned in despatches. He was buried with full military honours in the cemetery at Etaples. The stopping of all leave and recall of those already on leave gave promise of a move, but Easter was spent still in billets, and strenuous training and inspections were all that followed.

Lieut.-General Sir C. Monro, Commanding the First Army, inspected the Cavalry Division at this time. To prevent congestion behind the Army, the Cavalry Division was moved at the beginning of July to billets in the Amiens area. The offensive on the Somme led to the advance of the cavalry in the middle of July, when the Division concentrated near Mametz. The offensive of the Fourth Army took as its objective the capture of Longueval, Bazantin le Petit and Trones Wood, the 1st and 3rd Cavalry Divisions in conjunction with the 2nd Indian Cavalry Division concentrating on Beiordel. The holding up of the Bazantin le Petit and Longueval line by the enemy brought about a prolonged stay in bivouac near Querrieu, where training was continued until the Third Battle of Ypres. Working-parties were provided by the cavalry to assist the infantry. August brought a move west, the Regiment marching to the Ypres salient again. Passing Bailleul, the centre of the winter billets 1914–15, quarters were found at Longroy. The General Officer Commanding Fourth Army at this time presented Sergeant K. W. Stevens with the Military Medal, in recognition of his gallant devotion in attending to the wounded after the withdrawal of the working-parties on more than one occasion. No opening for the cavalry presenting itself during these operations, the Division was again withdrawn towards the sea, to prevent congestion, and training again followed in the district around Ault, north of Dieppe, only to be back again at the beginning of September to take part in operations under General Sir H. Rawlinson, Commanding the Fourth Army. Marching towards the scene of operations and counter-marching towards the sea grew monotonous, and the end of September found the Regiment again near the sea at Hesdin.

The year 1916 will be remembered as that of the Battle of the Somme, and for the introduction of Tanks in modern warfare.

Air-raids by Zeppelins, which were perpetrated over the British Isles in the previous year, were now of regular occurrence, and were carried beyond the East Coast, penetrating over London and the Midlands, where attacks were launched upon our great industrial centres.

The year was also marked by overtures on the part of Germany towards peace, and the intervention of President Wilson, of the United States of America.

CHAPTER XI

1917

THE band instruments now arrived from home to give promise of brighter things. Training during the first quarter of the New Year at Longvillers was much interfered with by hard frost and snow. The Pioneer Battalion continued its work on the St. Pol-Arras line, reliefs being sent up periodically, otherwise the monotony of a life of inaction was unbroken.

Regimental-Sergeant-Major Talbot was at this time gazetted a 2nd Lieutenant in the Royal Berkshire Regiment.

The equipment of the Hotchkiss detachment and the return of surplus equipment into store at the Base heralded the approach of a move, and on March 22 orders were received that the Regiment was to be in readiness to move at eight hours' notice, in the event of the cavalry being required by the First Army.

The formation of the Hotchkiss detachment consisted of one man and one horse per Troop, with three horses and two men per Squadron as horse-holders and pack-leaders ; two men and two horses per Squadron for ammunition packs.

April brought a move from Longvillers to Renty, where the dismounted party left by rail for the forward area to take part in the First Battle of Arras. The Brigade concentrated at Fruges, marching from there via Crepy to Monchy-Cayeux. The attack by the First and Third Armies opened on April 9, when the 1st Cavalry Division was to be connected with the First Army operating north of Arras, while the 2nd and 3rd Divisions operated with the Third Army to the south of Arras. The 2nd Cavalry Brigade, supporting the 1st Cavalry Brigade, reached St. Nicholas, where delay in launching the attack by the infantry prevented the advance of the Cavalry Division for some time. Heavy falls of snow impeded the advance, the roads in places being impassable. At the time of these operations the Cavalry Corps was commanded by Lieut.-General C. T. McM. Kavanagh, C.V.O., C.B., D.S.O., while Major-General R. L. Mullens, C.B., commanded the 1st Cavalry Division, and Brig.-General D. J. E. Beale-Browne, D.S.O., was in command of the 2nd Brigade.

48

The part played by the mounted troops in these operations
proved to be only in support of the infantry, and a return to
billets brought the monotony of training back again. The
Pioneer Battalion employed by the 46th Infantry Division
was put in to hold positions from time to time during the summer
months, and suffered some casualties. Corporals T. Wake and
H. A. Hollingsworth were awarded Military Medals for conspicuous conduct while working with the Battalion, and medals
for " Long Service and Good Conduct " were awarded to the
following :—

> Regimental Sergeant-Major Barrett.
> Farrier-Staff-Sergeant Old.
> Farrier-Staff-Sergeant Rutherford.
> Quartermaster-Sergeant Sabey.
> Saddler-Staff-Sergeant Wear.
> Sergeant Knight.
> Private Cole.
> Private Hamil.

The Military Medals were presented to the recipients by the
General Officer Commanding 2nd Cavalry Brigade.

A Commemoration Service in connection with the commencement of the fourth year of the War was attended by
representatives of the Regiment at Headquarters of the First
Army on August 5, when the troops were addressed by General
Sir Henry Horne, K.C.M.G., Commanding that Army.

A move to the sea and into camp came at the beginning of
September, the Regiment marching by Samer and Condette
after leaving the Bethune district.

Training followed for some months, a working-party remaining
behind and being attached to the Fourteenth Corps. October again
saw the Regiment on the march, but the cavalry were not required,
and a return was made to the billeting area by the end of the
month. A Pioneer Battalion was made up from the Brigade,
augmented from the 6th Dragoon Guards and the North Somerset
Yeomanry, and was attached to the Fifth Army, Major
Forsyth, M.C., being in command of the Company supplied
by the Regiment, assisted by Lieutenant. A. G. W. Harris.

The whole of the cavalry concentrated during the second week
in November in the Peronne area, preparatory to taking part
in Sir Julian Byng's attack on the Hindenburg Line.

CHAPTER XII

HINDENBURG LINE

November 20.

A T the commencement of these operations the following
were serving with the Regiment :—

REGIMENTAL HEAD-QUARTERS STAFF

Lieut.-Colonel H. S. Sewell, D.S.O., Commanding.
Captain R. J. F. Chance, M.C., Adjutant.
Captain F. A. Dunham, Quartermaster.
Captain Duffy, Medical Officer.
Lieutenant A. P. Williams, Assistant Adjutant.
Lieutenant J. B. P. FitzGerald, Intelligence Officer.
Lieutenant D. G. Williams, Signalling Officer.

" A " SQUADRON	" B " SQUADRON
Captain H. de G. Warter.	Captain D. G. F. Darley.
Lieutenant J. A. Aizlewood.	Captain C. F. Farley.
Lieutenant L. F. Marson.	Lieutenant A. M. Odling.
Lieutenant L. E. Misa.	Lieutenant G. A. Cattley.
Lieutenant W. N. Reeve.	Lieutenant B. St. V. Emsell.
Lieutenant R. A. Radclyffe.	Lieutenant J. Rawle.

" C " SQUADRON

Captain J. W. Aylmer.
Captain R. G. Fetherstonhaugh.
Lieutenant C. H. Pillman.
Lieutenant H. S. Green.
Lieutenant M. O'Donnell.
Lieutenant W. O. Cobbett.

OFFICERS FOR SPECIAL DUTIES

Lieutenant A. G. W. Harris; Lieutenant J. F. Sanderson;
Lieutenant H. S. L. Bedwell; Lieutenant G. E. de Pass.
Other Ranks : 583. Horses : 564.

The object of the operation undertaken by the Third Army,
under Sir Julian Byng, was to break the enemy's system by a *coup
de main* with the assistance of the Tanks, and to pass the Cavalry
Corps through the gap thus made, with certain definite objectives.

The 5th Cavalry Division was to move by Marcoing and
Masnières and thence north-east, followed by the 2nd Division; the
1st Cavalry Division by Ribecourt, east of the Bois des Neuf,
and both sides of the Canal de l'Escault, in order to turn Noyelles,
Cantaing, and Fontaine, and help the infantry to capture them.
The 2nd Brigade, the leading Cavalry Brigade of the 1st Cavalry
Division, were ordered, as soon as the infantry had gained their
final objectives, to assemble behind the Bois des Neuf.   The 5th
Dragoon Guards were temporarily attached to the Brigade, their
objective being to cross the Canal de l'Escault by the Marcoing
lock-bridge, work up northwards along the east bank of this canal,
and in conjunction with the advance of the 2nd Cavalry Brigade
seize in succession the crossings over the Canal de l'Escault.

Three sections of Tanks were placed under orders of the General
Officer Commanding 2nd Cavalry Brigade to deal with the
villages of Noyelles, Cantaing, and Fontaine.   The delay of the
advance of the infantry at Flesquières on the west, and the
5th Cavalry Division being checked at Masnières on the east,
led to the failure to force a gap except on the very narrow front
between Cantaing and the Canal de l'Escault.   It was through
this gap that Captain de Warter pushed his Squadron on a
front of barely a thousand yards, on his right the whole of the
east bank of the canal being in the hands of the enemy and on
his left the village of Cantaing still holding out.   It was so
late in the day that the Tanks allotted to the 2nd Cavalry Brigade
were not employed to deal with the village, and " A " Squadron,
having inflicted considerable damage, were skilfully withdrawn
in spite of attempts of enemy infantry to cut them off, both
from Cantaing and from the east bank of the canal.

The holding up of the infantry in Cantaing made the advance
of Captain de Warter with " A " Squadron a difficult one, while
on his right the Canal de l'Escault was still in enemy's hands
and heavy fire was brought to bear upon him from that direction.

Leading the advance of the Brigade, Captain de Warter, with two Troops of " A " Squadron, pushed on towards his objective, leaving the other two Troops to mask Cantaing. Galloping forward, a party of the enemy with four ammunition wagons were surprised, the whole party being shot or captured. Farther on, another party of dismounted Germans were charged by Captain de Warter at the head of his two Troops with like result. Meanwhile the enemy were collecting on the canal bank and advancing through the woods in the rear of " A " Squadron. Captain de Warter gave the order to withdraw, which was successfully carried out, he himself being killed during the retirement. (See Biographical Notes.) Lieutenant Pillman covered the retirement of " A " Squadron, the command of which had devolved upon Lieutenant Radclyffe, with a force from the Reserve Squadron, from the direction of Cantaing. It is impossible to estimate the number of prisoners taken during these operations, as they were passed back to the infantry by Captain de Warter, but they must have been between fifty and sixty. Two machine guns were also brought in, and considerable casualties were inflicted upon the enemy in the Escault valley, chiefly by machine-gun fire, when the ammunition column was surprised, and by rifle fire in the Bois des Neuf, and with the sword when the two Troops charged under Captain de Warter. The Germans had a battery in the village street at Cantaing, and the village was held by machine guns.

On the appearance of Captain de Warter's troops on their left rear, the enemy started running back from the village to the north, but were rallied by their officers and subsequently returned. It appeared that if the enemy had not been in strength on the east of the Escault Canal, it would have been possible to push the advance and to turn the village of Cantaing from the east. Lieutenants Aizlewood and Marson, both having their horses shot under them, returned to the main body after dark with a dismounted party and a machine gun. Our casualties during these operations amounted to four killed, four wounded, and six missing. Killed : Captain H. de G. Warter, Corporal Murray, Privates Hutchinson and Savage. Immediate awards on the field were : Bar to the D.S.O. to Lieut.-Colonel H. S. Sewell, D.S.O.; M.C.s to Lieutenants J. A. Aizlewood, C. H. Pillman, and L. F. Marson; and Medals to Sergeants E. F. Loads, A. E. Sutherland, and Lance-Corporals G. Kenyon and C. Hayes,

Privates R. West, W. H. Humphries, and A. W. Jeffries. Following this action the Brigade, assisted by the 7th Dragoon Guards, supported the infantry defending Noyelles, the 16th Middlesex and three Companies of the Royal Fusiliers holding the village. A counter-attack was made by the enemy at daybreak on November 21, but the line was restored in a couple of hours, Cantaing being captured by the 1st Cavalry Brigade. A return to camp held little promise of rest and refit, the Brigade standing-to to assist the infantry if necessary. The Divisional General visited the Regiment and conveyed the thanks of the Commander-in-Chief to them for the part they had played in the actions of the 20th and 21st.

A dismounted Battalion from the Brigade was now formed to assist the work of the infantry, the 4th Dragoon Guards supplying seven officers and two hundred other ranks and two Hotchkiss detachments per Squadron. The Battalion was taken up in support of the 120th Infantry Brigade and later attached to the 121st Infantry Brigade, and ordered to attack Bourlon Wood. This order was subsequently cancelled, and the Battalion returned to camp at Metz-en-Couture, after four days and nights of intense cold and exposure. Captain R. J. F. Chance left the Regiment to join the 1st Rifle Brigade on transfer, and the duties of Adjutant were assumed by Lieutenant R. Gordon-Munro. Captain Chance had served continually with the Regiment since August, 1914, save for the time he was incapacitated through wounds.

The beginning of December saw the formation of another dismounted Battalion from the Brigade, which was placed under the command of Lieut.-Colonel H. S. Sewell, D.S.O., while a second Battalion was formed from the Brigade, and a Company supplied from the 4th Dragoon Guards under Lieutenant Pillman.

These were used in occupation of a line of trenches supporting the front line near Heudecourt. Many transfers were at this time made to the infantry and commissions granted from the ranks of the cavalry, while a considerable number of horses were detailed to be sent to Egypt. A return from Bray to the camp at Doingt came at Christmas time, and it was found that during the absence of the Brigade all woodwork and anything that could be burnt had been removed by other occupants of the huts. The Brigade having to " stand to " on December 25, Christmas festivities were kept on the following day.

CHAPTER XIII

1918

THE year opened in very severe weather, with hard frost, the Brigade again undergoing a period of training, being in reserve in the Beaumetz district. A dismounted Battalion was again formed in the middle of January to relieve the Battalion from the 1st Division. This proceeded to the front line, Lieut.-Colonel Sewell, D.S.O., being in command, with Captain R. Gordon-Munro as Adjutant.

In March of this year it was decided that the 1st Cavalry Division was to become the Mobile Reserve to the Nineteenth Corps and was to be employed working on rear defence, each Brigade finding a Pioneer Battalion to be billeted in the vicinity of its work, and should the emergency arise, the horses to be brought up to the Battalions, whereas, if the position demanded it, the Battalions would be moved up, dismounted, to wherever required. By way of entertainment a Divisional Cinema at this time visited the Regiment. St. Patrick's Day was celebrated as usual. The opening of the Second Battle of the Somme, and the violent attack of the Germans on the Third and Fifth Armies, again brought the cavalry to the move. The Pioneer Battalion vacated the Doingt area and took over the 9th Brigade area at Devise. A good deal of marching and counter-marching followed, while the Brigade was kept in support of the infantry. The Somme was crossed at St. Christ, and the Brigade was brought up to support the Seventh Corps, which was sore pressed. Dismounted Battalions again were brought into use, and the gap between the Third and Fifth Armies was filled. The Dismounted Column was under the command of Brig.-General Beale-Browne, D.S.O., while the 2nd Brigade Dismounted party was commanded by Lieut.-Colonel H. S. Sewell, D.S.O. The enemy on our immediate front during the early stages of the battle had taken Bray, and pushed forward to Chippilly and Morlancourt, and the woods to the north of those places. The line held by the Divisional Dismounted Column under

54

General Beale-Browne ran from Sailly Laurette to Treux, his left at the latter place being in touch with the right of the Third Army at Ribemont. The 9th Lancers and the 8th Hussars moved forward under orders from General Beale-Browne, whose head-quarters were established on the main Corbie-Bray Road. The 4th Dragoon Guards occupied a strong position on the spur between the Somme and the Ancre on the north-west of Vaux-sur-Somme. The village of Sailly Laurette was occupied by Lieut.-Colonel Sewell, D.S.O., the 5th Dragoon Guards being attached to his command for the operation. Owing to the massing of the enemy, it was found impossible to advance beyond the village. Bouzencourt was held until the Cavalry Division was withdrawn and the line taken over by the Anzacs.

During the night the 1st Cavalry Division withdrew from the position covering the Anzacs, and crossed to the south of the Somme, where for some days they occupied a line from Bouzen-court-Hamel towards Marcelcave. Much reconnaissance work was done towards the south to keep touch with the troops on the right, and much of this work fell to the lot of the 4th Dragoon Guards. Here 2nd Lieutenant G. E. de Pass distinguished himself and was awarded the D.S.O.

During the operations between March 21 and 31 the Regiment lost eight men killed (see Casualty List) and Lieutenants Emsell, Courage, and Odling wounded, with forty-five other ranks wounded and thirteen missing.

The first fortnight of April was spent in refitting and training, while the Regiment was withdrawn from the line, but was required to be in readiness to reoccupy forward positions at short notice. Lieut.-Colonel H. S. Sewell, D.S.O., was at this time given command of the 1st Cavalry Brigade, while the command of the 2nd Cavalry Brigade devolved on Brig.-General A. Lawson, C.M.G., D.S.O.

Major E. M. Dorman succeeded to the command of the Regiment. Honours were bestowed upon 2nd Lieutenant G. E. de Pass, D.S.O.; Captain C. F. Farley, M.C.; Captain and Adjutant R. Gordon-Munro, M.C.; Captain J. Aizlewood received a Bar to his M.C.; Sergeant Harris, D.C.M.; Squadron-Sergeant-Major Barrett, D.C.M.; Corporal E. Bowley, M.M.; Corporal H. Stanton, Italian Bronze Medal for Military Valour.

An American officer, Lieutenant Rushing, was at this time attached to the Regiment as Medical Officer.

The summer passed without any incident of note. Several moves up to positions of readiness behind the front in anticipation of advances by the Infantry led to disappointment; but events were now moving quickly. The Germans had launched their final great offensive against Paris and had, after desperate fighting, been held up. Everyone was wondering when the long awaited counter-attack was to begin. By the beginning of August all was ready.

On the night of August 7 the Cavalry Corps was moved up through Amiens to the east, the 1st Cavalry Division moving into a position of readiness just south-west of Villers-Bretonneux, behind the 5th Australian and 2nd Canadian Divisions.

At early dawn on August 8 the battle of Amiens began. The Infantry attack met with but little resistance. The 1st Cavalry Brigade on the north and the 9th Cavalry Brigade on the south of the Villers-Bretonneux–Nesle railway followed on their heels. These Brigades soon overtook and passed the advancing Infantry, assisted them in reaching their final objectives and surprised the enemy reserves before any counter-attack could be launched. The success of General Rawlinson's Army was greatly helped by the action of the divisions of the Cavalry Corps on this day. How complete this success was, history has shown.

Over 1,200 prisoners were taken by the 1st Cavalry Division, and spoils included a railway train full of returning leave men, who promptly held up their hands, a fully equipped hospital, and a vast number of guns and material which it was impossible to check.

During the day the Regiment was with the 2nd Cavalry Brigade acting in support, but towards evening they were engaged towards Caix. In the neighbourhood of this place the Division settled down for the night after a long and stirring day. An advance of over 10 miles had been made and the Germans had been badly shaken. The 8th of August will always be remembered by those who took part in this attack as the day in which the Cavalry, after so many months of waiting, had at last come into their own.

On the following day reconnaissances were pushed forward to locate the enemy's exact position. Reconnoitreing patrols from " A " Squadron were driven back by machine gun fire from Rosières and the old outer defences of Amiens.

Later, the Canadian Infantry attacked, the 2nd Cavalry Brigade supporting them. A considerable number of casualties occurred amongst the Brigade Staff, while the 9th Lancers suffered very heavily in the endeavour to move forward against Fouquescourt, but few casualties were caused in the Regiment. Lieutenant R. G. Giddings, North Somerset Yeomanry (attached), being killed and twenty-three other ranks being wounded ; twenty-three horses killed and thirty-three wounded. After some few days the Cavalry were ordered back to a position near Amiens. On the return march the Brigade was bombed from aeroplanes, one bomb falling between the rear of the Regiment and the head of the 18th Hussars, two men being wounded and seven horse casualties. A move forward was made from the "Concentration Area" during September to clear up the situation at Courcelles-le-Comte, about half-way between Arras and Bapaume. The Cavalry were to take advantage of any opportunities presenting themselves after the forward movement by the 3rd Infantry Division. Officers' patrols were sent forward under Lieutenants Gillett and Rawle. The report of the former satisfactorily cleared up the situation, and it was found that the infantry had not reached the line of the railway—their first objective. This work was carried out with the loss of Sergeant E. W. Harris, and fourteen casualties, while five horses were killed and eleven wounded.

Towards the end of September the Cavalry were again on the move eastwards towards St. Quentin, past Peronne, where the Australians had won fresh laurels, across the old British front line, which had been held by the dismounted 1st Cavalry Division in the early weeks of the year, just prior to the German offensive the previous March.

The Hindenburg Line, with its wonderful galleries and dugouts, was crossed at Bellicourt. (In the tunnel here, where the canal runs underground, some gruesome remains, the result of one of our heavy shells, gave rise to all manner of horrible stories as to the disposal by the Germans of their dead.)

The early days of October saw the advance pushed towards Le Cateau, the Cavalry Division being ordered to push through the infantry toward the objective—the line east of Villers-Outreaux-Serain—Premont—Fresnoy le Grand. The 1st Division led the cavalry advance, supported by the 2nd Cavalry Division. The 9th Brigade leading, the 2nd Cavalry Brigade echeloned to the left and the 1st Cavalry Brigade to the right. As soon as the barrage lifted the 2nd Brigade were ordered to push on La Motte, and thence to Ponchaux, which was reached towards midnight of October 8. The 9th Lancers, operating on the left, were ordered to send a Squadron forward to the north-west of Serain to clear up and report on the situation. The rest of the 9th Lancers moved at the same time to Les Folies, south-east of Serain, and the 4th Dragoon Guards followed on and halted in the valley south-east of Les Folies. An "Observation Post" was sent to the high ground south-east of Les Folies, to watch the movements of the 9th Lancers. The latter Regiment reported that Serain was clear of the enemy, and that Elincourt was said to be held by machine guns, and that the 9th Lancers were moving towards Iris. The 4th Dragoon Guards were moved up to a point west of Serain, where they were met by machine and artillery fire from the direction of Elincourt. Sheltering under cover of a ridge, a Troop of "A" Squadron was sent forward to get into touch with the 9th Lancers at La Lampe, south-east of Malincourt. Twelve Hun aeroplanes made their appearance and bombed and machine-gunned the Brigade. Lieutenant Radclyffe duly reported that the 9th Lancers were held up at La Lampe and the Deheries-Serain Road was strongly held by the enemy, and that our infantry held only the west half of Serain. No further movement by the cavalry was possible, as the infantry could not dislodge the enemy from its position on the Elincourt-Serain road, and the cavalry were withdrawn for the night to a position near Gouy. Next day brought the 1st Division to the support of the 3rd Division. The Dragoon Guards were detailed to act as left flank guard to the 3rd Division, having the Canadian Brigade on their right. The Regiment was, however, ordered to rejoin the 2nd Cavalry Brigade and were withdrawn for the night.

The advance on Le Cateau was carried out by the Thirteenth Corps, the Fifth marching on Neuvilly, the Fourth on Briastre. It was found impossible to carry out the projected scheme, and the Regiment was withdrawn to its former billets, to await further developments.

During October and early November the Cavalry continued to advance in a north-easterly direction, and on November 11 was in touch with the enemy to the south of Ath. At 11 o'clock on that day the "Cease Fire" sounded. The Armistice had been arranged. At the cessation of hostilities the Regiment was at Beloeil, about 10 miles north-east of Mons, the scene of the first engagement by the Regiment with the Germans in March, 1914.

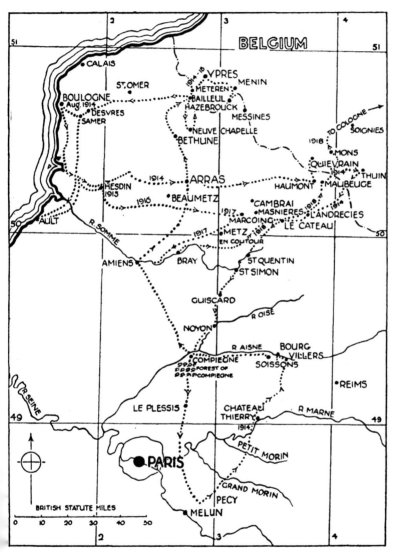

THE ROUTE OF THE REGIMENT.

1914–1918.

CHAPTER XIV

" INTO GERMANY "

THE 1st Cavalry Division withdrew to Peruwelz, whence, after a few days' halt, it led the advance of the British Army to the Rhine. Cologne was occupied on December 8. The Regiment took over the western ends of the two northern bridges across the Rhine, the Germans continuing to hold the eastern ends.

The Regiment occupied the Artillery Barracks in the town.

On December 18 Field-Marshal Lord Plumer inspected the Regiment as it crossed the Hohenzollern Bridge over the Rhine, at the head of the column of British Troops detailed to occupy the zone of German territory to the east of the Rhine.

Christmas Day was spent in the Artillery Barracks, while Divine Service was attended by the Regiment for the first time for some years in a Church—the English Chapel at Cologne.

The usual routine followed, and on January 16 H.R.H. the Prince of Wales, accompanied by the General Officer Commanding 2nd Cavalry Brigade, inspected the Regiment.

Two months later saw the return of the Regiment from active service, to be stationed for a time in Ireland. Sailing from Antwerp on April 27, Kingstown was reached via Tilbury and Holyhead.

In conclusion, it may be noted that the Regiment had been on active service continuously, from the first clash of the British with the enemy until the " Cease fire," a period of four years and three months.

One hundred and ninety-one Officers, N.C.O.'s, and Privates had given their lives.

OFFICERS—1914.

LIEUT. K. P. WALLIS.   CAPT. .... A.V.C. (ATTACHED).
2ND LIEUT. O. B. SANDERSON.   CAPT. C. L. DIGGORY.   LIEUT. A. WRIGHT.   2ND LIEUT. J. C. LEECH.
LIEUT. R. K. McGILLYCUDDY.   LIEUT. A. GALLAHER.
MAJOR C. GAUNT.   LIEUT.-COLONEL R. L. MULLENS.   CAPT. C. F. HUNTER.   CAPT. G. B. LAMONT.   CAPT. R. J. B. OLDREY.
LIEUT. S. G. SANDERS.   LIEUT. A. E. HICKMAN.
CAPT. H. S. SEWELL.   CAPT. AND ADJT. C. B. HORNBY.

Appendix I

List of Officers who landed in France with
the 4th (R.I.) Dragoon Guards
on 16th August 1914.

LIEUT.-COLONEL.
R. L. Mullens.

MAJORS.
A. Solly-Flood, D.S.O.
G. T. M. Bridges, D.S.O.
C. F. Hunter.
R. Hutchison.

CAPTAINS.
H. S. Sewell.
C. B. Hornby.
R. J. B. Oldrey (Adjt.).
R. K. McGillicuddy.
G. H. FitzGerald.
A. Wright (Special Reserve 4th Dragoon Guards).
J. Hardress Lloyd (Reserve of Officers).

LIEUTENANTS.
A. Gallaher.
J. W. Aylmer.
Sir A. E. Hickman, Bart.
O. B. Sanderson.
D. G. F. Darley.
S. J. W. Railston (Indian Army).
H. L. Jones (13th Hussars).

2ND LIEUTENANTS.
R. G. Fetherstonhaugh.
F. B. B. Pigeon.
J. Holman.
R. Gordon-Munro.
R. J. F. Chance.

QUARTERMASTER.
F. A. Dunham (Hon. Lieut.).

Appendix II

BIOGRAPHICAL NOTES

OFFICERS

Aizlewood, J. A., Lieut. Joined Regt. 10.11.'14. Mentions: 8.11.'17. M.C. 18.1.'18. Capt. 12.12.'17. Bar to M.C. 5.4.'18.

Ambrose, W. J. L., 2nd Lieut. 21.9.'14. W. 5.3.'15. Transfd. home, 19.3.'15.

Aylmer, J. W., Lieut. Mentions: 17.2.'15 ; 1.1.'16. Capt. 5.5.'15. M.C. 14.1.'16. G.S.O. (3rd gr.) 14th Army Corps 3.2.'16. O.C. " C " Squadron, 7.9.'16.

Bedwell, H. S. L., Lieut. 22.2.'17 (promtn.).

Bell, F. W., V.C., Capt. 30.12.'14. Transfd. home, 1.4.'15.

Bernards-Bryan, C. G., 2nd Lieut. 18.10.'15. Transfd. 7th L.N.Lancs. 26.5.'16.

Berry, W. A., 2nd Lieut. 27.11.'14. T. Lieut. 18.9.'15. Lieut. 25.2.'16. Transfd. R.F.C. 14.3.'17.

Bethune, Lieut.-General Sir E. C., K.C.B., C.V.O., Col., Dir. Gen. T.F. (W.O.) '14–'17.

Boosey, R. G., 2nd Lieut. 1.12.'14. Mention: 13.3.'15. K. in A. 24.5.'15.

Bridges, G. T. M., Major 14.8.'14. W. in A. 28.10.'14. Mentions: 8.10.'14; 22.6.'15; 30.11.'16; 7.11.'17. Croix de Guerre (France) 11.10.'14. Lieut-Col. to Command 4th Hussars 3.9.'14. Attached Belgian Army 18.10.'14. W. in A. 11.4.'15. T. Brig.-Gen. 1.7.'15. C.M.G. 23.6.'15. T. Maj.-Gen. (Commdg. 19th Div.) 13.12.'15. Brevet-Col. 1.1.'16. G.C. Order of Leopold (Belgium) 24.9.'16. Croix de Guerre (Belgium) 13.3.'16. Maj.-Gen. 1.1.'17. Tempy. Lieut.-Gen. 8.4.'17. W. in A. 20.9.'17. C.B. 1.1.'18. K.C.M.G. 1.1.'19.

Brown, O., Lieut. 9.9.'14. K. in A. 24.4.'15. Transfd. from 7th Lancers (I.A.).

Butler, F. H., Lieut. 23.11.'14.   W. in A. 7.5.'15.   Rej. 1.1.'16.
   Invld. home 18.1.'17.

Cary, R. A., 2nd Lieut. 13.12.'17.   Lieut. 7.10.'17.

Carton de Wiart, A., V.C., Capt. 7.12.'14.   Camel Constblry., Somali-
   land F.F.   W. in A. '14.   Joined Regt. March '15.   2nd i.c. Regt.
   3.3.'16.   O.C. L.N. Lancs. Regt. (S. Batt.) April '16.   O.C. 8th
   Gloucester Regt. June '16.   G.O.C. 12th Infy. Brig. Jan. '17.
   G.O.C. 105th Brig. April '18.   G.O.C., 113th Brig., 12.11.'18.
   Brevet-Maj. 11.'17.   Brevet-Lieut.-Col. 6.'17.   Temp. Brig.-
   Gen. 14.11.'18.   Mentions: 13.11.'16;   9.1.'17;   7.11.'17;
   20.2.'15.   D.S.O. 15.5.'15.   V.C. 8.9.'16.   Croix de Guerre
   (Belgium) 8.3.'18.   Ordre de la Couronne (Belgium) 21.4.'17.
   C.M.G. 3.6.'18.   A.D.C., June '17.   W. in A. 19.11.'14; 10.5.'15;
   23.7.'16; 25.10.'16; 8.11.'17; 22.4.'18.

Cattley, G. A., 2nd Lieut. 17.5.'15.   Lieut. 8.8.'15.   Transfd. 6th
   Dragoon Guards 23.3.'19.

Chance, R. J. F., 2nd Lieut. Lieut. 15.8.'14.   W. in A. 3.11.'14.
   Mention: 23.6.'15.   M.C.   Lieut. 5.5.'15.   Capt. 1.11.'16.
   Adjt. 3.1.'16.   Transfd. 1st Rifle Brigade 31.11.'17.   5th A. School
   '18.   W. in A. 22.4.'18.

Chapin, H. S., Capt. 24.11.'14.   Transfd. 17th Batt. Liverpool Regt.
   30.11.'16.

Clarke, H., 2nd Lieut. 27.11.'16.   Invld. home 14.7.'18.

Cobbett, W. O., Lieut. 26.10.'17.   Transfd. from 3rd Dragoon Guards.
   A.D.C. to G.O.C. 1st Cav. Bde. 15.12.'18.

Collyer, H. A., 2nd Lieut. 13.8.'16.   Temp. Lieut. 1.7.'17.   Attachd.
   Tank Corps 20.12.'17.   Transfd. to Tank Corps 10.1.'18.

Courage, P. M., 2nd Lieut. 24.12.'17.   Lieut. 29.7.'17.   M.C. and Bar.
   W. in A. 24.3.'18.

Crawford, J. B. H., Lieut. Transfd. from N. Somerset Yeomanry
   29.9.'18.

Cullen, R. V. D., 2nd Lieut. 5.1.'18.   Lieut. 1.11.'18.

Darley, D. G. F., Lieut. 15.8.'14.   W. in A. 20.10.'14.   Capt. 6.11.'15.
   Mention: 13.11.'16.   R.F.C., May '18 to May '19.

Davison, D. S., Lieut. 13.10.'14.   W. in A. 31.10.'14.

Delmege, J. O'. G., 2nd Lieut. 14.3.'15.   Lieut. 12.12.'14.   W. in A.
   24.5.'15.   Died of W. 27.5.'15.

Dent, G., 2nd Lieut. 23.5.'15.   Lieut. 5.8.'15.   M.G.C. 25.2.'16.
   M.C. 1.4.'18.

Devin, C. E., 2nd Lieut. Transfd. from Essex Yeomanry 29.4'.18.
   Lieut. 29.12.'18.

Digby, T. H., 2nd Lieut. 12.6.'15. Transfd. to Motor Battery Cavalry Corps 21.9.'15.

Dorman, E. M., Capt. Restored to Est. from N. Irish Horse 5.8.'15. Temp. Major 28.3.'16. Actg. Lieut.-Col. (C.O.) 29.9.'16–20.11.'16. Instr. 6th Res. Regt. 4.11.'17. Actg. C.O. 2.5.'18. Mentions : 30.4.'16. M.C., Brevet-Major, D.S.O.

Dunham, F. A., Lieut. Mention : 30.11.'15. Hon. Capt. and Q.M. 1.7.'17.

Elmslie, K. W., Lieut. 23.9.'14. K. in A. 3.11.'14.

Emsell, B. St. V., 2nd Lieut. 29.11.'14. W. in A. 28.3.'18. Lieut. 4.9.'17.

Farley, C. F., 2nd Lieut. 9.1.'15. Lieut. 30.11.'15. Mention : M.C. Capt. 1.11.'16.

Fetherstonhaugh, R. G., Lieut. 25.8.'14. W. in A. 31.10.'14. Capt. 5.8.'15.

FitzGerald, G. H., Capt. K. in A. 13.9.'14.

FitzGerald, J. B. P., 2nd Lieut. 23.5.'15. Lieut. 3.1.'16. Mention : 17.12.'18.

Forsyth, F. R. G., Capt. M.C. Transfd. from Seaforth Highlanders 23.12.'16. W. in A. 30.10.'17.

Gallaher, A., Lieut. W. in A. 24.8.'14. Prisoner of W. Reported for duty 5.9.'14. W. in A. 13.5.'15 ; 20.8.'16 ; 6.9.'16 ; 8.10.'18. Mentions : 30.11.'15 ; 13.11.'16 ; 20.8.'16. Capt. 5.5.'15. D.S.O. 1.1.'17. Médaille de Sauvetage Belgium) 24.2.'18. R.F.C. 25.10.'18. Rejoined Regt. 28.6.'18. Egyptian Cavalry 1916. Adjt. Dorset Yeomanry 1.1.'17–1.4.'17. Spec. Mention, M.C.

Gibb, J. H. O. (Revd.), Lieut. 28.10.'14. W. in A. 10.5.'15.

Giddings, R. G., 2nd Lieut. Transfd. from N. Somerset Yeomanry 30.5.'18. K. in A. 9.8.'18.

Gillett, P. G., 2nd Lieut. 26.10.'17. M.C. 1.4.'18.

Gordon-Munro, R., 2nd Lieut. Lieut. 1.4.'15. A.D.C. to G O.C. 37th Infy. Div. 1.10.'15–1.12.'15. W. in A. 8.9.'14. Adjt. and Capt. 30.11.'17. M.C. 27.3.'18.

Green, H. S., 2nd Lieut. 22.2.'17. K. in A. 4.4.'18. D.C.M.

Greenhill, T. W., 2nd Lieut. 9.12.'14. Lieut. 12.12.'14. Mention : 30.4.'16. K. in A. 12.2.'16.

Hardress-Lloyd, J., Capt. A.D.C. to G.O.C. 1st Cav. Bde. 10.10.'14. A.D.C. to G.O.C., 29th Div. in Gallipoli 15.5.'15–1.1.'16. O.C. 1st R. Inniskilling Fusiliers 1.5.'16–1.1.'17. Tank Corps 1.4.'17. Brig.–Gen. '17. Mentions : 6 times. D.S.O. and Bar '17, '18. Légion d'Honneur '17.

Harris, A. G. W., 2nd Lieut. 31.7.'16.

Harrison, G., Lieut.   Transfd. from 14th Hussars '14.   Transfd. to Infy. '15.

Heron, W. F., 2nd Lieut. 14.3.'15.   Mention: 15.4.'16.   K. (accidentally) 3.4.'16.

Hickman, Sir A. E., Bart., Lieut. W. in A. 24.8.'14. P. of W. 24.8.'14. Capt. 5.8.'15.

Hine, V. T. G.   Capt. Transfd. from Essex Yeomanry 3.7.'18.

Hodgkin, H. S., Capt. Transfd. from 1st Cheshire Regt. 1.12.'14. Mentions: 5.4.'15; 25.6.'15; 29.1.'17; 22.12.'17. D.S.O. 26.6.'15.   O. C. 26th Notts and Derby Regt. 16.4.'16. W. in A. 26.9.'17. P. of W. 21.3.'18. Brevet-Major 1.1.'18.

Holman, J., 2nd Lieut. Died of W. 29.10.'14.

Honey, G. D., 2nd Lieut. 1.3.'15.

Hornby, C. B., Capt. W. in A. 20.10.'14. Mentions: 20.11.'14. D.S.O. 18.2.'15. Major 5.8.'15. G.S.O. (3rd gr.) W.O. 1.11.'16. Croix de Guerre 21.4.'17.

Hunter, C. F., Major. A.M.L.O. (Calais) 5.5.'15. D.A.A.G. Hdqrs. L. of C. 11.8.'15. A.A.G. Res. Army 23.6.'16. A.A. and Q.M.G. British Military Mission, G.H.Q. French Army 12.4.'17. Mentions: 8.10.'14; 30.4.'16; 9.4.'17. D.S.O. 2.6.'16. Brevet-Lieut.-Col. 3.6.'17.   Croix d'Officier, Légion d'Honneur (France) 17.12.'17.   Croix de Guerre (France) 1.1.'18.

Hutchison, R., Major. Brig.-Maj. 1st. Cav. Bde. 1.9.'14. G.S.O. (2nd gr.) 30.10.'14. G.S.O. (2nd gr.) G.H.Q. 11.1.'15. G.S.O. (1st gr.) G.H.Q. 28.10.'15. Brevet-Lt.-Col. 14.1.'16. G.S.O. (1st gr.) W.O. 5.2.'17. Brevet-Col. 3.7.'16. Temp. Major-Gen. 1.5.'17. Mentions: 20.11.'14; 5.11.'14; 30.11.'15; 1.1.'16. Ordre de la Couronne (Belgium) 24.2.'17. C.B. 28.12.'17. Croix de Guerre (Belgium) 11.3.'18. Commd. of Order of Crown of Italy 28.4.'19. D.S.O. 1915.   K.C.M.G. 1919.   D.S.M. (U.S.A.) 1918.

Jones, H. H., Lieut. Attchd. from 13th Hussars '14. W. in A. 28.10.'14. D.S.O. '16. Légion d'Honneur (France) 1.9.'14. Mentions: 5 times. Adjt. 13th Hussars 1.5.'16. 2nd i.c. 7th E. Lancs Regt. 1.11.'16-1.2.'18. O.C. 7th E. Lancs Regt. 1.3.'18-1.11.'18. O.C. 9th Welsh Regt. '19.

Kirkwood, J. C. M., Capt. From Res. of O. W. in A. 21.10.'14. 1st Life Guards 5.11.'14-13.9.'15. Attchd. to B.E. African F., 17th Bengal Lancers (I.A.) 1.12.'15-15.7.'16. D.S.O. '17. O.C. R.I.R. (T. Batt.) 1.10.'17. W.O. '18.

Lean, J. V., Lieut. 4.11.'14. Transfd. to R.G.A. '14.

Lillingston, E. G. G., 2nd Lieut. 21.12.'14. Army Signals 10.1.'17.
Lieut. 5.8.'15. Mention : 9.4.'17.

Loveridge, M. W., 2nd Lieut. Transfd. from Hampshire Regt.
31.10.'18. M.C. 1.2.'19.

Lovett, T. M., 2nd Lieut. 5.8.'15. Injured 5.9.'15.

McFarlane, J. G., Lieut. 18.11.'14. A.M.L.O. (Temp. Capt.).

McGillicuddy, R. K., Capt. G.S.O. (3rd gr.) 1.11.'15. D.A.A.G.
1.1.'17. A.A.G. at W.O. 1.9.'17. Mentions : 5.9.'14 ; 8.10.'14 ;
15.5.'17. D.S.O. 14.1.'17. Légion d'Honneur (France) 14.7.'17.
Brevet-Major 3.7.'17. Brevet-Lt.-Col. 1.1.'19.

McNeill, L. E., 2nd Lieut. Transfd. from N. Irish Horse 7.12.'14.
Lieut. 20.3.'16. Invalided 28.5.'17.

Marson, L. F., 2nd Lieut. 3.3.'15. Lieut. 7.11.'15. Mentions : M.C.
15.1.'18.

Mildmay, W. H. St. J., Capt. 9.1.'15. To Res. Regt. 7.4.'15.

Misa, L. E., 2nd Lieut. 3.2.'17. Lieut. 1.7.'17. W. in A. 20.11.'17.

Mullens, R. L., Lieut.-Col. G.O.C. 2nd Cav. Bde. 10.10.'14. G.O.C. 1st
Cav. Div. 24.10.'15. Mentions : 8.10.'14 ; 19.1.'15 ; 30.11.'15 ;
7.11.'17 ; 13.11.'16 ; 8.11.'18 ; 16.3.'19. Brevet-Col. 18.2.'15.
Col. 4.8.'15. Major-Gen. 21.12.'18. C.B. 1.1.'17. Croix de
Guerre (Belgium) 7.12.'18. Croix de Guerre (Avec Palmes)
(France) 1919.

Mullens, G. J. de W., 2nd Lieut. 24.11.'18. A.D.C. to G.O.C. 1st
Cav. Div. 30.11.'18.

Odling, A. M., 2nd Lieut. 3.2.'16. Lieut. 1.7.'17. W. in A. 30.3.'18.

O'Donnell, M., 2nd Lieut. 9.12.'14 (promtn.). W. in A. 24.5.'15.
Mentions : 30.11.'15. M.C. 14.1.'16. Lieut. 12.2.'16.

Ogilby, R. J. L., Lieut. 1914. Transfd. to O.C. 7th Norfolk
Regt. 11.4.'17. O.C. 2nd/14th London Regt. 4.9.'17.
B. Salonika E.F. 29.11.'17.

Oldrey, R. J. B., Capt. Adjt. of Regt. 1914. K. in A. 28.10.'14.

Oppenheim, R. W., Capt. Rej. Regt. 30.3.'17. D.A.A. and Q.M.G.
3.12.'17. A.A. and Q.M.G. 5.9.'17. Brevet-Major 28.12.'17.

Parker, N. A., 2nd Lieut. 29.7.'17.

Pass de G. E., Lieut. 27.7.'17. Mentions : 17.12.'18. D.S.O.

Pigeon, F. B. B., 2nd Lieut. 1914. Transfd. to Res. Regt. 1.12.'14.

Pilcher, A., Capt. Attchd. from 21st Lancers 3.1.'15. Rejd. 21st
Lancers 21.11.'15.

Pillman, C. H., 2nd Lieut. 17.10.'15. Lieut. 5.8.'15. Mentions: 18.1.'18. M.C. 18.1.'18. A.D.C. to G.O.C. 1st Cav. Bde. 18.4.'18.

Powell, H. O., 2nd Lieut. 29.10.'14. K. in A. 31.10.'14.

Radclyffe, R. A., 2nd Lieut. 22.10.'15. Lieut. 20.3.'17.

Railston, S. J. W., Lieut. Transfd. from 18th Bengal Lancers '14. K. in A. 1.11.'14.

Ramsay, A. FitzG., Capt. 20.9.'14. P. of W. 12.10.'14.

Ramsay, N., Lieut. 29.10.'14. K. in A. 3.11.'14.

Rawle, J., Lieut. 18.5.'15. Transfd. to Res. Regt. 27.7.'15. Rej. 26.10.'17.

Reeve, W. N., 2nd Lieut. Transfd. from 16th Lancers 3.5.'17. Mentions: 1.1.'17. M.C. Lieut. 3.11.'17. O.C. 2nd Signal Troop R.E. 20.8.'18.

Richardson, D. R., 2nd Lieut. Transfd. from 3rd Dragoon Guards 30.5.'18.

Rogers, G. C. B., 2nd Lieut. 10.5.'17.

Romer Williams, C., Lieut. Attchd. from G.H.Q. Intell. O. '14. A.D.C. to G.O.C. 1st Cav. Div. '16. Transfd. to Welsh Guards '16.

Rubie, J., 2nd Lieut. 9.2.'15. Transfd. from Royal Horse Guards. W. in A. 24.4.'15. Transfd. to R.F.C. 19.6.'15.

Sanderson, J. F., 2nd Lieut. 26.10.'17.

Sanderson, O. B., Lieut. W. in A. 29.8.'14. P. of W. 29.8.'14. Capt. 7.11.'15.

Sebright, G. E., 2nd Lieut. 1.12.'16. Lieut. 1.7.'17.

Sewell, H. S., Capt. Major 3.9.'14. Temp. Lt.-Col. 13.3.'15. G.O.C. 1st Cav. Bde. 7.4.'18. W. in A. 13.9.'14; 13.5.'15. Mentions: 20.11.'14; 5.4.'15; 7.2.'17; 17.12.'18. Croix de C. Légion d'Honneur 6.11.'15. D.S.O. 3.6.'15. Bar to D.S.O. 15.1.'18. C.M.G. 1919.

Sharpe, W. A., 2nd Lieut. 1.10.'14. Mention: 8.10.'14. W. in A. 20.10.'14. Lieut. 12.2.'16. Sec. to M.G.C. 20.3.'16.

Solly-Flood, A., D.S.O. Temp. Lt.-Col. 10.11.'14. Brevet-Lt.-Col. 18.2.'15. Lt.-Col. 5.8.'15. G.O.C. 35th Infy. Brig. 31.10.'15. Brevet-Col. 1.1.'17. Brig.-Gen., G.H.Q., 16.3.'17. Temp. Maj.-Gen. to command 42nd Infy. Div. 15.10.'17. Mentions: 20.11.'14; 15.6.'16; 13.11.'17; 17.11.'17; 17.12.'18. W. in A. 24.5.'15. C.M.G. 3.6.'16. Comdr. Ordre de la Couronne 26.7.'16. Croix de Guerre (Belgium) 8.3.'18. C.B. '18. Croix de Guerre (Avec Palmes) France '18.

Stanley, K. B., 2nd Lieut. 15.2.'18.   Lieut. 12.3.19.

Thwaites, M., 2nd Lieut.   W. in A. 3.11.'14.   Mentions : 17.2.'15.
M.C. 18.2.'15.   American Military Mission '16.

Tollemache, D. P., Hon., Capt.   From 7th Hussars 14.7.'15.   Brig.-
Maj. 2nd Cav. Bde. '15.

Turner, H., 2nd Lieut. 27.7.'17.   W. in. A 29.9.'17.   Temp. Lieut.
1.7.'17.   Lieut. 28.9.'17.   Disabled 9.5.'18.

Warter, H. de G., Lieut.   W. in A. 16.10.'14.   Capt. 1.11.'16.   K. in A.
20.11.'17.

Wickham, J. B., 2nd Lieut. 10.4.'16.

Williams, A. P., 2nd Lieut. 2.2.'16.   Lieut. 1.11.'17.   Actg. Adjt.,
Temp. Capt. 28.9.'18.   Mention : 17.12.'18.

Williams, D. G., 2nd Lieut. 12.6.'15.   Lieut. 5.8.'16.

Worlock, E. G., 2nd Lieut. 22.3.'15.   Lieut. 20.3.'16.   Temp. Capt.
27.12.'17.   Sec. to M.G.C. 1.10.'16.

Wright, A., Capt.   W. in A. 31.10.'14 and 24.5.'15.   Mention :
2.1.'17.

Wyllie, H. T., Capt. 17.11.'14.   K. in A. 24.5.'15.

TIDWORTH

1914.

Appendix III

CASUALTY LIST

OFFICERS, N.C.O.s, AND PRIVATES
KILLED IN ACTION
OR
DIED OF WOUNDS

1914  1918

OFFICERS: 16.   N.C.O.s and PRIVATES: 175.

"QUIS SEPARABIT."

1914.

Allen, W. H., Pte. . 1.11.'14
Baker, F. G., Pte. . 27. 9.'14
Baker, W. J., L.-Corpl 13. 9.'14
Beckett, H., Corpl. . 3.11.'14
Bloomfield, B., Corpl. 24. 8.'14
Calloway, W. J., Sergt. 3.11.'14
Carey, J., Pte. . . 17.11.'14
Carter, L., Pte. . . 16.10.'14
Chapman, F. C., L.-Cpl. 13. 9.'14
Coleman, A., Pte. . 3.11.'14
Connor, A., Pte. . . 3.11.'14
Cramp, E. W., Pte. . 20.10.'14
Cross, W., Pte. . . 24. 8.'14
Davis, T., Pte. . . 24. 8.'14
Drury, W., L.-Corpl. . 12.10.'14
Elmslie, K. W., Lieut. 3.11.'14
Fearis, F. C., Pte. . 10.10.'14
Fidler, B. L., Pte. . 24. 4.'14
FitzGerald, H., Capt. 13. 9.'14
Frey, W. G., Pte. . 2.11.'14
Good, S. C., Pte. . . 2.10.'14
Green, Z., Pte. . . 3.11.'14
Greenwood, A., Pte. . 3.11.'14
Hadley, G. D., Pte. . 12.11.'14
Hawes, J. E., Pte. . 24. 8.'14
Henry, J., L.-Corpl. . 1.11.'14
Hewson, T. G., L.-Corpl. 2.11.'14
Holman, J., 2nd Lieut. 29.10.'14
Horey, J., Pte. . . 3.11.'14
Hughes, O. T., L.-Cpl. 1.11.'14
Hunt, G. W., Pte.. . 1.11.'14
Johnstone, W., Sergt. 28.10.'14
Jones, A. F., S.Q.M.S. 6.11.'14
Jordan, F. D., Pte. . 18. 9.'14
Larkins, J., Pte. . . 21. 9.'14
Lee, P., Pte. . . . 1.11.'14
Leonard, W., Pte.. . 20.10.'14
McDonald, T., Pte. . 3.11.'14
McKenzie, A., Corpl. . 1.11.'14
Marvin, H., Pte. . . 3.11.'14
Monk, J. W., Pte. . 3.11.'14
Mummery, J. W., Pte. 1.11.'14
Noakes, J. W., Pte. . 18.11.'14
Oldrey, R. J. B., Capt. 28.10.'14
Page, A. H., Pte.. . 24. 8.'14
Partridge, L., Pte. . 1.11.'14
Pitman, J., L.-Corpl. . 3.11.'14
Powell, H. O., 2nd Lt. 31.10.'14
Puttick, A., Corpl. . 28.10.'14

Railston, S. J. W., Lt. 1.11.'14
Ramsay, N., Lieut. . 3.11.'14
Richardson, C., Pte. . 1.11.'14
Roake, E. W.,Pte. . 10.10.'14
Rosser, J. M., Pte. . 28.10.'14
Rush, A., Pte.. . . 24. 8.'14
Sampson, G., Pte.. . 28.10.'14
Savoury, H., Corpl. . 13. 9.'14
Skates, E. F., Pte. . 1. 9.'14
Smith, B., Pte. . . 23. 9.'14
Smith, P., Pte. . . 3.11.'14
Snow, J., Sergt. . . 28.10.'14
Stewart, E., Pte. . . 1.11.'14
Stubbs, W. C., Sergt.. 20.10.'14
Taylor, S. S., Pte.. . 1.11.'14
Thomas, B., Pte. . . 8. 9.'14
Ticehurst, W., L.-Cpl.. 6. 9.'14
Upton, G., L.-Corpl. . 4. 9.'14
Watts, S. T., Pte.. . 24. 8.'14
Westcott, S. B., Pte. . 7.11.'14
Whiteman, E. G., Sergt. 6. 9.'14
Worley, W., Pte. . . 28.10.'14
Young, A., Pte. . . 1.11.'14

1915.

Arnold, A., Pte. . . 30. 5.'15
Barclay, E., Pte. . . 7. 5.'15
Boosey, R. G., 2nd Lt. 24. 5.'15
Bourlet, W., Pte. . . 10. 5.'15
Branch, C. W., Pte. . 4. 6.'15
Brown, O., Lieut.. . 24. 4.'15
Caselton, F., Pte. . . 13. 5.'15
Chilton, F. A., Pte. . 4. 3.'15
Delmege, J. O'.G., Lt. 27. 5.'15
Evans, T., Pte. . . 4. 3.'15
Everitt, W., Pte. . . 24. 5.'15
Gilpin, J., Pte. . . 7. 5.'15
Gray, R., Pte.. . . 14. 5.'15
Hammond, C. D., Pte. 24. 8.'15
Hayes, A., Corpl. . . 5.10.'15
Hockley, F., Corpl. . 24. 4.'15
Honnor, A. E., Pte. . 10. 5.'15
Hunter, J. W., Pte. . 24. 5.'15
Hutton, H. P., Pte. . 23. 5.'15
Keeley, J., Pte. . . 10. 5.'15
King, A. E., Pte. . . 30. 9.'15
Long, J. T., Pte. . . 14. 5.'15
Lowe, F., Pte.. . . 10. 5.'15
Mahoney, E. J., L.-Cpl. 7. 5.'15
Merry, W. F., Pte. . 24. 5.'15

Moore, E., Pte. . . 29. 5.'15
Moore, J., Pte. . . 24. 5.'15
Parkhouse, H., Corpl. 10. 5.'15
Perry, F., Pte.. . . 30. 5.'15
Shaw, H. W., Pte. . 24. 5.'15
Shoulbridge, A. J., Pte. 24. 4.'15
Stocker, W. A., L.-Cpl. 10. 5.'15
Stuttard, R. A., Pte. . 20. 5.'15
Trueman, E. W., Sergt. 10. 5.'15
Venn, W., Pte. . . 13. 5.'15
Waghorn, A. H., A.-
Sergt. . . . . 17. 5.'15
Waite, F., Sergt. . . 19.11.'15
Warwick, W. H., S.-S. 11. 5.'15
Wastell, W. A., Pte. . 9. 1.'15
Williams, J., Pte.. . 24. 5.'15
Woodward,G. H., L.-Cpl. 8. 6.'15
Wright, W. J., A.-Sergt 24. 9.'15
Wroe, A., Pte.. . . 24. 5.'15
Wyllie, H. T., Capt. . 24. 5.'15
Young, J., Pte. . . 5. 3.'15
Young, W. S., Pte. . 11. 5.'15

1916.

Bagnall, W., Pte.. . 14. 3.'16
Boston, J. C. S., Pte. . 24. 9.'16
Cassidy, V. S., Pte. . 29. 1.'16
Chandler, W., Pte. . 11. 2.'16
Clapp, H., Pte. . . 7. 1.'16
Ellery, J., Pte. . . 6. 1.'16
Elliott, F. S., Pte. . 5. 1.'16
Gibbs, S. W., Pte.. . 8. 1.'16
Greenhill, T. W., Lieut. 12. 2.'16
Heron, W. F., Lieut. 3. 4.'16
Knight, H. E., Pte. . 12. 2.'16
Kolbe, D. W., L.-Corpl. 30. 1.'16
Merrick, W. G., Pte. . 1. 8.'16
Nicholas, H., Pte.. . 1. 8.'16
Nicholson, W., Pte. . 7. 8.'16
Pegler, A. J., Sergt. . 7. 8.'16
Porley, G., Pte. . . 2. 3.'16
Robinson, C. C., Pte.. 1. 8.'16
Robinson, T. R., Pte.. 29. 1.'16
Swingler, C. A. B., Pte. 24.10.'16
Taylor, W., Pte. . . 16. 5.'16

1917.

Barnard, S. S., Pte. . 26. 3.'17
Broad, W., Pte. . . 20. 1.'17
Cotterell, F., Pte.. . 7. 9.'17
Downer. C., Pte. . . 1.12.'17

Doyle, P., Pte. . . 1. 7.'17
Duerdoth, F. S., Pte.. 23. 1.'17
Gregory, A., Sergt. . 20.11.'17
Harvey, F. G., Pte. . 1. 7.'17
Huff, J. W., Pte. . . 26.12.'17
Hutchinson, T., Pte.. 20.11.'17
Kirk, F. W., Pte.. . 7. 9.'17
Lloyd, J., Pte. . . 2. 7.'17
Murray, W. G., Corpl.. 21.11.'17
Nicholls, W. D., Corpl. 7. 3.'17
Savage, J. T., Pte. . 21.11.'17
Scott, J., Pte.. . . 3. 7.'17
Smith, R. R., Pte. . 3. 7.'17
Turkington, W. H., Pte. 21. 9.'17
Warter, H. de G., Capt. 20.11.'17
Wilkin, C., Sergt.. . 20.11.'17
Wright, T. H., Pte. . 1. 7.'17
Young, A. G., Sergt.. 2. 5.'17

1918.

Ardern, R., Pte. . . 21. 8.'18
Bennett, F., Pte. . . 21. 3.'18
Birchley, A. W., Sergt. 9.11.'18
Brearton, J., Pte. . 25. 3.'18
Bromley, A., Pte.. . 13. 3.'18
Clark, A., Pte.. . . 28. 3.'18
Dilly, A. J., Pte. . . 25. 3.'18
Doyle, J., Pte. . . 21. 8.'18
Ellis, E. G., Pte. . . 27. 3.'18
Gaunt, W., Pte. . . 22. 3.'18
Giddings, R. G., 2nd Lt. 9. 8.'18
Glidewell, M., Pte. . 10.11.'18
Green, H. S., Lieut. . 4. 4.'18
Harris, F. W., Sergt.. 21. 8.'18
Hughes, T., Pte. . . 27. 3.'18
Ives, F. W., Pte. . . 21. 3.'18
Kimbrey, H. W., Pte. 2. 4.'18
Loads, E. F., Sergt. . 26. 3.'18
McHale, A., Pte. . . 22. 3.'18
Mahoney, P., Pte. . 5.11.'18
May, W., Pte.. . . 15. 4.'18
Morris, N., Pte. . . 21. 3.'18
Osborne, A. H., Pte. . 2.11.'18
Palmer, W., Pte. . . 9. 8.'18
Roberts, H. C., Pte. . 27. 3.'18
Shepherd, H., Pte. . 4.11.'18
Simmons, E., Farr.-
Sergt.-Maj. . . . 26. 7.'18
Taylor, J., Pte. . . 2. 4.'18
Trory, F. R., Sergt. . 22. 3.'18
Wallington, R., Pte. . 15.10.'18

Appendix IV

THE TOY BAND.

A Song of the Great Retreat.

Words by Sir HENRY NEWBOLT.

Music by Sir RICHARD PAGET.

PUBLISHERS:- CURWEN & SON, 24 BERNERS ST.W.1.

1 Drear-y lay the long road,

drear-y lay the town, Lights out and nev-er a glint o' moon.

Wear-y lay the stragglers, half a thousand down, Sad sigh'd the weary big Dra-

goon. "Oh! if I d a drum here to make them take the road a-gain.

72

Oh! if I'd a fife to wheedle Come, boys come! You that mean to fight it out

Wake and take your load a-gain. Fall in Fall in! Fol-low the fife and drum.

Fol-low the fife and drum.

Vivace.

1st time f 2nd time ff

loco

Appendix IV

"THE TOY BAND"

A Song of the Great Retreat

Dreary lay the long road, dreary lay the town,
    Lights out and never a glint o' moon.
Weary lay the stragglers, half a thousand down,
    Sad sighed the weary big Dragoon :
" Oh ! if I'd a drum here to make them take the road again.
    Oh ! if I'd a fife to wheedle : Come, boys, come !
You that mean to fight it out, wake and take your load again,
    Fall in ! Fall in ! follow the fife and drum ! "

" Hey ! but here's a toy shop, here's a drum for me,
    Penny whistles too, to play the tune !
Half a thousand dead men soon shall hear and see
    We're a band ! " said the weary big Dragoon.
Rubadub ! Rubadub ! Wake and take the road again,
    Wheedle-deedle-deedle-dee ! Come, boys, come !
You that mean to fight it out, wake and take your road again,
    Fall in ! Fall in ! Follow the fife and drum !

Cheerily goes the dark road, cheerily goes the night,
    Cheerily goes the blood to keep the beat.
Half a thousand dead men marching on to fight
    With a little penny drum to lift their feet.
Rubadub ! Rubadub ! Wake and take the road again,
    Tweedle-deedle-deedle-dee ! Come, boys, come !
You that mean to fight it out, wake and take your road again,
    Fall in ! Fall in ! Follow the fife and drum !

As long as there's an Englishman to ask a tale of me,
    As long as I can tell the tale aright,
We'll not forget the penny whistle's Wheedle-deedle-dee !
    And the big Dragoon a-beating down the night.
Rubadub ! Rubadub ! Wake and take the road again,
    Wheedle-deedle-deedle-dee ! Come, boys, come !
You that mean to fight it out, wake and take your load again,
    Fall in ! Fall in ! Follow the fife and drum !

Appendix V

THE BATTLE-HONOURS

In Army Order 129/1924 (April, 1924), List III, the following Battle-Honours were awarded to the Regiment :—

" Mons "

" Le Cateau "

" Retreat from Mons "

" Marne, 1914 "

" Aisne, 1914 "

" Messines, 1914 "

" Armentières, 1914 "

" Ypres, 1914, '15 "

"Frezenberg "

"Bellewaarde "

" Somme, 1916, '18 "

" Flers-Courcelette "

" Cambrai, 1917 "

" St. Quentin "

" Rosières "

" Amiens "

" Albert, 1918 "

" Pursuit to Mons "

" France and Flanders, 1914–18 "

The awards printed in Capital letters are those selected to be borne on the Standard and appointments.

1914  1918

Printed in the United Kingdom by
Lightning Source UK Ltd., Milton Keynes
140988UK00001B/8/A